Frontline Airline

Troop Carrier Pilot in World War II

The insignia of the 1st Troop Carrier Command, which was worn on the epaulets, in board of the rank. *Vincit qui primum gerit* — "He who attacks first, conquers."

Frontline Airline

Troop Carrier Pilot in World War II

John R. (Bob) Lester
Lieutenant Colonel, USAF (Ret.)

Sunflower University Press®
1531 Yuma (Box 1009), Manhattan, Kansas 66502-4228 USA

Printed in the United States of America on acid-free paper.

ISBN 0-89745-179-1

Cover: A 5th Air Force C-46 in operation in the Philippines, 1944-1945.
(Photo by Ed Miltz, courtesy Jeff Ethell, Front Royal, Virginia.)

Edited by Sandra J. Rose

Layout by Lori L. Daniel

Dedicated to those who bet
their lives to preserve freedom.
In the future, whenever this bid is
necessary, may they hold a Royal Flush.

Contents

Prologue

For me it began with this:

AVIATION CADET EXAMINING BOARD
HEADQUARTERS
Hartford Armed Forces Induction District
555 Asylum Street, Hartford, Conn.

February 13, 1943

SUBJECT; Call to Duty.

1. You will report at this headquarters on February 26, 1943 at 8.00 A.M. for shipment as a private Air Corps Unassigned for Pre-Aviation Cadet Basic Training. You are hereby informed that your deferment has been revoked by the Secretary of War.

2. When reporting, it is suggested that you bring with you a limited

amount of luggage including toilet articles, and personal effects. You will be furnished all necessary clothing at your first station.

3. Complete and return the lower portion of this order in the enclosed envelope. Do this immediately.

4. Failure to comply with the instructions in paragraph 1, will render you liable for trial by court-martial.

E. B. THOMAS
Captain, A.C.
President.

And before it was all over, many things happened, some tragic, some funny. Now, as I review 50 years later — and from this time perspective a selective memory process is probably at work — overall there is more humor than pain. An alternate explanation could be that these writings still contain the residuals of a time when the United States of America was truly *UNITED*.

In that time everyone eagerly sought a role in what was viewed as the defense of freedom. Ration books were there, and even cigarette commercials supported the effort with slogans like "Lucky Strike Green went to war." Bandages were rolled by church groups, and scrap metals were collected by the Boy Scouts. High school bands were at the train stations to bid the boys "Goodbye." Block air-raid wardens patrolled the night, while "plane spotters" scanned the skies by day. A soldier or sailor standing on a street corner resulted in civilian drivers offering a ride, even competing with each other for the privilege. A uniformed patron in a bar never bought a drink, for the nearest civilian picked up the check or it was "on the house."

USO clubs were always full. There was "Rosie the Riveter," "Kilroy," and the posters "Loose Lips Sink Ships" and "Buy War Bonds!" The music of the time revealed predominant themes: "I'll Be Seeing You," "Don't Sit Under the Apple Tree with Anyone Else but Me," "The White Cliffs of Dover," "Till Then." Humor was in "Sad Sack" and the Bill Mauldin cartoons, and the serious came from Ernie Pyle, war correspondent, killed in action just a mile from where I parked my C-46 on Ie Shima.

Everyone contributed as best he could; there were no protesters. Rather, a blue star in the window identified the home of a current serviceman, while a gold star proclaimed a death in defense of liberty. Anyone classified 4F was devastated; some even committed suicide, because they were being left out.

This was a generation nurtured in the Great Depression. People had learned to survive hardship as a matter of course. All were accustomed to work. The teenagers of the day were responsibly self-sufficient. Needs, not wants, dominated behavior. Material waste was minimal.

If your parents had been lucky enough to find a job, they taught you that if you could get one, do your best and hope that your employer stayed in business.

Common sense was the norm, and in today's parlance, everybody was "street wise." No one had learned how to quit.

If you had jumped into a foxhole but one second after your predecessor, complaining about the descending shells or bombs, the standard response was, "You should'a been here when it was rough!"

The USA of that time, steeled by the trials of the Depression, was tough and accustomed to battling the odds. Japan had really "awakened a sleeping giant."

And there was naiveté, for the world was only sparsely viewed and remained distant, with access to radio or Movietone News in the local theater (admission 15 cents). Until Europe was overrun and England was in peril, few paid attention. War movies then offered the reassuring theme that "right" (translated, "America") always won in the end. Add to the above the sense of immortality, which is characteristic of the very young, and you can imagine that the above order was seen as an invitation to adventure.

And so it was, for in retrospect, there are memories of things we could never have imagined. In my mind's eye, I can still look back through the Plexiglas dome of a Pathfinder C-47 and see planes — hundreds, stacked up and laterally — blackening the sky, the entire assault force dependent on the judgment in our cockpit. And there was the view of the Pacific covered with ships as far as I could see — multiple Task Forces: stately battleships; carriers with decks covered with planes; slick and mean cruisers; destroyers doing constant pirouettes.

There was the sudden icing, when the plane didn't want to fly. Head hunters in New Guinea, their hair a fiery red to indicate they were looking for a mate, a shrunken head hanging as from a necklace. Coral beaches, all once beautiful, but some covered with shattered palm stumps and rusting wrecks of tanks and landing craft. Plane crashes followed by fire, too often someone you knew well. The Fleet being pounded off Okinawa, while sitting in the entrance of a burial crypt on Ie Shima, counting the "Divine Wind" suicide strikes — those we got and those who got us. Black sand on Iwo, and my first experience with P-61 Black Widows, when at night they jumped a “Bogey” while being vectored from the Iwo tower.

And later, there was the white-tailed Betty, a Japanese twin-engine bomber, as it stopped to refuel on the way to the Japanese surrender, and the fireworks as ack-ack exploded and rained down on Okinawa to celebrate the end, driving us back to the burial crypts to avoid the falling shrapnel. And, of course, the return home. The embarrassment in the New York hotel lobby when I asked for a package of gum and was offered a whole carton, something not available at all to civilians (I took it and passed some out to everyone).

And then to meet my wife again, after all the time apart. How shy and uncertain I was when I realized how long I had been without warmth or gentleness. Once again, the real world began to come into focus.

Fifty years have passed. The world has been good to me. Now I can fully appreciate how fortunate I have been. Yet, all along, I expected it to come out OK. Don’t the good guys always win?

My very first set of official orders looked like this:

RESTRICTED

SPECIAL ORDERS) AVIATION CADET EXAMINING BOARD
: FORT DEVENS, MASSACHUSETTS
NUMBER 20 :) February 27, 1943

Par. 1. Pursuant to authority contained in IA letter, HFSC, dated February 6, 1943, subject: “Shipment of Men Qualified for Aviation Cadets,” the following named Privates, Air Corps Unassigned, WP this date by rail to the Army Air Forces Technical Training Command, Atlantic City, New Jersey, reporting upon arrival thereat to the Commanding Officer, AAFTTC, for assignment to the class in pre-Aviation Cadet basic training:-

FR ACEB HARTFORD, CONNECTICUT

[*In this group I was number 57 on a list of 94. With the additions from Fort Devens (83), Fort Rodman (16), Camp Edwards, Massachusetts (12); Camp Langdon, New Hampshire (9); Fort Adams, Rhode Island (3); Presque Isle, Maine (2); Rutland, Vermont (1), these were 220 college boys headed for the unknown.*]

TDN FD 31P 431-02A 0425-23. The QM will furnish the necessary rail transportation. The privates mentioned in this order were last rationed to include supper, February 27, 1943.

Captain Errold B. Thomas, AUS is designated as Train Commander for the movement of the troops quoted in this order.

Service records and allied papers on these men are in possession of the train commander.

BY COMMAND OF MAJOR GENERAL MILES
Stanley Powloski
Lt. Colonel, Inf.
President of Board

AVIATION CADET EXAMINING BOARD
FORT DEVENS, MASS.

RULES AND REGULATIONS GOVERNING THIS RAIL MOVEMENT

1. No one will de-train without specific authority.

2. Rail property will in no way be defaced.

3. Seats, aisles and cars in which Cadets are riding will be kept clean and orderly.

4. Papers, bottles, fruit and candy wrappers will not be thrown about the cars.

5. Cadets will not partake of alcoholic beverages.

6. Cadets will not stand on the platform between cars, lean out the window, or ride at the rear of the train.

7. Cadets will not enter parts of the train where they are not authorized.

8. No letters will be mailed enroute.

9. Any other instructions deemed necessary and proper by the Officer in Charge will be followed strictly.

Any violations of the above regulations or evidence of misconduct will be reported by the Officer in Charge upon arrival. Any reports of violations will be cause for severe disciplinary action and possible disqualification as an Aviation Cadet.

HARDING C. NEWMAN
1st Lieut. F.A.
Asst. Post Rctg. Officer
Recorder for the Board

[*Note: The Lieutenant Colonel was from the Infantry and the 1st Lieutenant from the Field Artillery. It was some months before we even saw anyone wearing wings.*]

And from this point on, my place on this planet and my time were at the discretion of others and/or events over which I had no influence. What follows is my account of people (some real, others with fictitious names), places (some identifiable, others indistinguishable in their sameness), and events as I recall them now.

Chapter 1

Basic Training

Incidents: Ground	74th Training Wing, 710th Training Group
Atlantic City, New Jersey	Army Air Forces Training Command
February-March 1943	(AAFTC)

We unloaded from the train in Atlantic City, as new recruits, right off the college campus. We were met by a PFC, clearly power mad, who herded us into trucks for a trip to the Claridge Hotel. The whole process seemed a strange way to start learning to fly airplanes. And it was, for we began to get in shape by running up and down stairs to the twelfth floor several times a day, often with full pack, gun, and gas mask — ready for combat.

Reveille was officially at 0600, but we started at 0400, because our company commander was a Regular Army Puerto Rican corporal, who could not read very well. He started roll call at the top with the "A"s and sometimes got as far as the "G"s before he would get stuck. If someone was foolish enough to prompt him, since we were all at attention, he would start again at the beginning of the list. Within two weeks, he could get through all the names in one and a half hours, still offering an unintelligible product, but everyone had finally learned not to prompt. During the first two weeks of this morning ritual, three potential cadets had stabbed themselves in the stomach with their own mess knives and were carted off, never to be seen again. Even in those instances, the corporal started at the beginning of the list once again.

A favorite tactic was to call a "gas drill" between 0100 and 0200, which required that we fall in, fully equipped with gas mask on, after which we would run around the parking lot, sometimes in the rain or snow. We played what amounted to a game of roulette: at times we might forget clothes and fall in with just an overcoat. Too often, however, this would be the time that there would be a spontaneous march on the Boardwalk for the next four hours. In sleet and snow, without clothes, that was an unpleasant stroll! Frequently, the Boardwalk was so coated with ice that we had to lock arms to keep from falling. Even then, whole platoons would at times tumble into a laughing, cussing pile. Despite the Army's attempt to turn us into infantry types with Basic Training in the swamps of New Jersey, it never succeeded in getting our heads out of the clouds.

On arrival we had been given an introductory lecture by a full three-stripe buck sergeant, who was in charge of the hotel that housed 1,200 GIs. There were not enough line officers to go around. I saw but one 1st lieutenant, and he at a distance, during the entire time in Basic. Thus, in fact as well as in know-how, the Regular Army prewar sergeants ran the induction process.

The lecture as I remember went like this:

> Smart-ass college kids! Flying fuckers! Flying horseshit! You'll never live to see an airplane, because I'm going to bust your asses before you can leave here. The ones I can't break will be putting in for Section 8s.

I might add that he did try to keep his promise and even succeeded in a few cases. Fortunately, he had so many personnel to deal with that he wasn't able to concentrate on many individuals. There was safety in the numbers, but that often also meant that a foul-up by one doomed a whole platoon to punishment.

In retrospect, the most dangerous aspect of Basic Training was the likelihood of exposure to contagious diseases. Several died of meningitis. I got a first-hand sample of the medical situation.

I was assigned to the midnight shift guarding the boilers of one of the hotels, which housed troops. The weapon I carried was a night stick, hardly sufficient to ward off a determined saboteur. There were four boilers, each operating at full output, and the heat generated was impressive. For the first hour, the heat was tolerable, but as time passed it seemed to get worse. I even read the steam gauges in an effort to account for the apparent change of temperature. By the second hour, whatever the cause, I knew that I was ill. According to the manual, I began the prescribed call: "Corporal of the Guard, Post 23." The magnitude of the post number should indicate that this wasn't a setup designed for speed of response. Toward the beginning of the fourth hour, my relief finally appeared. I was told I looked like hell and had better head for sick call, which began at 0800, some four miles down the Boardwalk. I started off, holding on to the railing most of the way to keep my balance, and got there by 0730. There were at least 200 GIs, some who really looked ill, seated in two lines of folding chairs. I was directed to take a chair and wait. At 0900 a corpsman stuck a thermometer in my mouth as he came down the line. At 1000 he reappeared to collect readings. He looked at mine, shook his head and observed, "Over 105; man you're sick. You need to see a doctor."

At 1230 I did see a physician, one who was dressed not in "pinks," which was the standard Army officer uniform, but in "purples," something I'd never seen before or since. Maybe it was the fever, but others told me that the physicians actually did wear that color in that time and place. The doctor took one look, said, "Measles, hospital" and moved on. By 1400 I was in a hospital bed and don't remember much else except that I was out in two weeks and on my way to a College Training Detachment. I do know that no one sabotaged the boilers while I was on duty.

Chapter 2

Preflight Training

Incidents: Air & Ground
Gettysburg, Pennsylvania
April-June 1943

55th College Training
Detachment, AAFTC

With Basic Training completed, we were transferred to a College Training Detachment, which had several functions:

1. Academic refresher for those who needed to improve in math, English, etc.
2. Initial exposure to flight with emphasis on aerobatics, which weeded out those inclined to air sickness before they reached the classification stage.
3. An opportunity to learn and practice military lore and customs.
4. A holding arrangement, which made possible systematic funneling of candidates into the training command.

In terms of the national interest, the College Training Detachment was an effective device. From a personal viewpoint, the arrangement was a dream.

First, there was the setting of Gettysburg College itself, a picturesque campus, surrounded by history, where leading figures of the Civil War had trod. We walked past ivy-covered buildings to classes and each weekend ranged over the battlefield on foot. During the week, we flew over the area and used historic places like Little Round Top as aerial checkpoints. This exposure to the battlefield, both on the ground and from the air, kindled an interest in the Civil War, which later, for years, became a pleasant, high-grade preoccupation of mine.

Second, I was able to quiz out on all basic subjects and thus was allowed to select alternatives. I chose geopolitics, which was taught by a German refugee professor who was able to make us really understand the political cross-currents, particularly with respect to both Germany and the Soviet Union. As a result of his teachings, years later, I was not surprised that Russian anti-aircraft batteries did their best to knock down our squadron's planes when they inadvertently crossed the 38th parallel on instruments trying to find Seoul, as we first went in to occupy Korea. Nor was I surprised in conversations with Russian pilots in Tokyo at the war's end when they wondered why we were all going home, while they had every intention of remaining in service indefinitely. They anticipated that there would be much to do in Japan, if only as the result of the efforts of the Soviet intelligence agencies' KGB and GRU agents who were trying to foment strikes and riots. They obliged in pointing out some of these agents at work in front of General Douglas MacArthur's headquarters. And since then there have been 50 years to collect data on the Soviets and their intentions. Before the Soviet Union collapsed, it was considered an evil empire.

A third benefit of the College Training Detachment was that this was the beginning of a membership in a fraternity with those who wholeheartedly aspired to the same goals. We began to "hangar fly," performing maneuvers with our hands, such that even a distant observer of the conversation could identify an Immelmann or a chandelle. It is from such exposure that there results the saying: "A pilot is just a plane guy with a special air about him."

And fourth, there was the air. We went up daily in Cubs and Aeroncas with civilian instructors who vied with each other to set records for multiple-turn spins. Regularly, they pushed these planes to the limits of their aerobatic envelope, always with an aspiring cadet as passenger. Legally, we were not supposed to land or take off, yet in the air we were encouraged to engage in aerobatics. Never were we allowed to fly solo. Our instructors had several hundred private flying hours, and we looked up to them as elite. In retrospect, they were patient and considerate, never raising their voices in rebuke, as was the way of my subsequent military flight instructors. In sum, they were in love with flight and were simply trying to pass that skill on as they had previously to civilian students. By contrast, the military method of training was to push us to the limit, emotionally and physically, on the assumption that this would eliminate the faint of heart.

Soon after I had graduated, my civilian instructor at Gettysburg came to the base where I was stationed for military Advance Pilot Training with the goal of achieving flight officer. Ironically, although he had been a competent pilot in light planes with hundreds of hours, he was killed landing a Curtiss twin-engine AT-9 while in training for transition to medium bombers. The AT-9 was not forgiving, but that's another story.

In many ways, of all the assignments before the war ended, Gettysburg was the most relaxed and pleasant in all respects. I could understand why President Eisenhower chose that setting for his retirement.

Incidents: Ground
Nashville, Tennessee
July-August 1943

Squadron F-3, Nashville
Army Air Classification
Center, AAFTC

Classification: the process where it is decided whether one is put together physically, intellectually, and emotionally in proper proportions, such that it is worth the risk in time and expense to try to convert the individual from private through aviation cadet to an officer and gentleman with *Silver Wings.*

All manner of tests were given: verbal; motor performance, with emphasis on manual dexterity; reaction time, with and without distraction; projective; psychiatric interview; and complete physical evaluation, with emphasis on vision — color and depth perception. When not being tested for something, there was physical education: again, tests of capacity for long-distance running, push-ups, chin-ups, and all-around physical stamina. There was a production-line quality about the whole process, which culminated in an appearance before the Cadet Board to receive the final judgment that would determine (from that time perspective) one's entire future life or, as it turned out for too many, one's mode of death.

The stay in Nashville was a strange, unreal hiatus, which has left only vague, unconnected memories, perhaps because of the hectic pace of the classification process. It was certainly a pattern of hurry-up for the next test, only to have to wait in another line.

It was always too hot, and when we could, we crawled under the barracks to stay out of the sun. But we never could escape the heat. And there were flies everywhere. Mess halls were surrounded with fly traps, which were emptied daily, completely filling 6x6 trucks with the winged carcasses.

As for people, I recall an old Regular Army prewar first sergeant, who, when observing a potential cadet candidate standing in the company street, bellowed from his office window: "Damn it soldier, don't stand there — *DO* Something!" And there was a tac (tactical) officer, a retread, who actually lectured us for two hours on the topic of the virtue inherent in shining shoes. He insisted that it was this procedure alone that kept him on balance and able to face the stress of military life. For the first time, I had encountered an individual misplaced as an officer. Unfortunately, there were to be many more.

Just two days before I was to report before the Board for evaluation, I was admitted to the infirmary for what turned out to be sunstroke. The technician duly recorded a rise in blood pressure, which didn't go down when he told me about it. All I could think about was spending the war shining shoes. A flight surgeon took a quick look, then directed me to lie down. In a half hour he was back, and with a smile threw me back into the stream of candidates that flowed toward the Classification Board.

The measurements from all the tests were collated and expressed as "Sta 9s" — a euphemism for summarizing and predicting a candidate's suitability for success under three categories: pilot, navigator, and bombardier. A 9 represented the highest rating, and although they never said, I would guess that anything below a 7 resulted in disqualification. Initially, we had been given the option of choosing one of the three categories, which they said would be a factor in our selection. My day of judgment finally came, but it was before a "Special Board." Naturally, I read all manner of negative meanings into that word "Special" as I waited my turn. A sergeant opened the door to the room and beckoned to me.

I marched straight and stiff toward the major, who as chairman, was flanked by captains and a 1st lieutenant or two. In the prescribed manner I saluted with:

"Private, Lester, John R. Reporting as ordered, Sir."

The major responded, "Private, it says here that you have expressed the wish to be a bombardier. Is that correct?"

"Yes, Sir."

The major, a pilot, said, "But why would you pick bombardier?"

I could answer honestly, "There was no compelling reason; it just seemed like a good idea at the time, Sir."

He continued, "We have a problem with your choice. We are going to

Cadet barracks time out.

The author as a U.S. Army Air Corps cadet.

need a lot more pilots than bombardiers. You have scored 9s on all three, which says we think you can succeed in any of the positions. We want you to try to become a pilot, and if you don't make it, you can always try for bombardier. If you will sign this paper I hold, which says you promise to do your best to become a pilot, you will be put on orders for transfer to Maxwell Field to begin Cadet Training."

My answer, "Yes, Sir," provoked smiles from the entire Board as I eagerly signed the form.

The major concluded with, "You are no longer a private, but now you are an aviation cadet. You are dismissed, Mister."

And he almost beat me to the parting salute.

I later learned that the "Special Board" was held for cadets who had scored high enough to be pilots, but who had made another choice.

Incidents: Ground
Maxwell Field, Montgomery, Alabama
September 1943

Squadron 3, Field, 1X,
Army Air Forces Preflight
Training Center, AAFTC

Maxwell Field was where for the first time we got to wear the shoulder patch and hat emblem with the silver propeller flanked by gold wings that designates an aviation cadet. There, the emphasis was on the decorum expected of an Air Corps officer.

It seemed as though we were at perpetual attention. Even while running, we would be reminded to keep "heads up, eyes, ahead." Dining as new arrivals, we learned to eat "square" meals, which meant precision movements from plate to mouth, with eyes straight ahead, preventing a view of what was on one's plate. Throughout the stay at Maxwell there was always a table leader who directed the proceedings involving the clockwise passing of dishes, and the granting of permission for conversation. I remember a new arrival who reached for a slice of bread immediately after grace. He withdrew his hand to examine the puncture wounds produced by four forks. Nothing was said, yet his experience was a lesson to us all. The food, served by busy waitresses, was always excellent, and we were always hungry. Seconds were common, and usually there would be requests for more. When the portions ran out, the response of the waitress was definitive and final: "Ain't no more!" In later years I found this phrase very useful, even with my own children.

There were classes on Morse code and aircraft recognition, as well as on more academic subjects. Physical exercise in the form of calisthenics and cross-country running were daily events. And we marched — by flight, by squadron, by group — parade after parade. We went everywhere looking straight ahead, and thus we hardly ever saw the dignitaries on the reviewing stand for whom the parade was conducted. The officials must have loved parades, because we had so many in such a short span of time. Then there was always retreat, the daily flag-lowering, another excuse to parade.

I made the grade as a cadet officer, which entitled me to wear a sword. Again, on parade, this symbol of command was impressive when wielded properly in salute from right shoulder to chin and point to the ground at "Pass in Review." Maxwell Field was the only place where I ever had anything to do with a sword until a Samurai sword showed up in the cockpit of a kamikaze plane, along with an unexploded bomb, that had plowed into a

C-46 parked next to mine on Ie Shima.

Tours for infractions were the norm at Maxwell, and there were countless opportunities. This meant an hour of marching, during what should have been free time, with a parachute bouncing against your legs. Someone in the flight would neglect to shine the back of a belt buckle, or overlook dust that would smudge the white glove of an inspecting officer when he touched some out-of-the-way place in the barracks, like the top of a window ledge or the shade on an overhead light — some place that could be reached only by the use of a ladder, which he had brought along for that purpose! *Anyone's* infraction was often made *everyone's* infraction in that particular flight, so we would all get "gigged" — punished — which resulted in walking tours on weekends in lieu of a pass to town. Consequently, none of us saw very much of the city of Montgomery.

There may have been method in this tactic, however, for the one vivid memory I have of Maxwell Field stems indirectly from the aftermath of weekend passes. Someone had done something on pass, we never found out what, that led to his expulsion from the Cadet Corps. We were roused out late one Saturday night, long after taps. All cadets, in full dress uniform at parade rest, listened to the charges against a hapless cadet, who, while on pass, had behaved in a manner "unbecoming an officer and gentleman." To the somber beat of a drum he was summarily expelled. At the conclusion of this grave ceremony, the Corps was called to attention for dismissal, which was always preceded by an exchange of salutes between the corps commander and the flight leaders, at least one of whom had gotten drunk while on pass. This inebriate was identified, when at the occasion of the salute he briskly brought his sword hilt up to his chin and then losing his grip, higher still until it landed on the barracks roof behind the flight. I remember this event as the only time I have ever seen silent pandemonium, for the Corps remained, at least overtly, at attention, while the sword clattered noisily down the sloping roof and landed on the ground with a thud seemingly as loud as a thunderclap. The following evening, the Corps was once again in formation to witness the expulsion of the cadet who had lost his sword.

If there is a need for defense of the kind of rigid discipline that was imposed during Cadet Training, one can point to the fact that on completion of the training, the silver wings awarded virtually guaranteed that the wearer would not abuse his authority, since he had learned what it was like to be "low man on the totem pole." GIs typically respected officers with wings, but were not always nearly as accepting of ground officers, who too often were said to be "chicken shit."

Because every pilot commands the plane, regardless of who is with him, the habit of assuming total responsibility has to be developed and cultivated. In the tightest of situations, the pilot is expected to be a disciple of reasonable behavior. I recall too many radio transmissions controlled almost *sotto voce* from pilots who, having exhausted every option, realized that they were about to crash. And so Cadet Training, begun at Maxwell Field, was designed to produce the man from Kipling's *If* who would "keep his head, when everyone about is losing theirs."

Chapter 3

Primary Flight Training

Union City, Tennessee
October-November 1943

Squadron D, Embry Riddle
Field, AAFTC

Finally, we were there — a flight line with real airplanes just waiting to be flown. Dozens of PT-23s — a variant of the PT-19 — with low wings, dual open cockpits, and big radial engines sat expectantly, ready to take to the air. We could see the planes from the bus windows as we passed, heading for the barracks, but typical of the Army Air Corps, we were then under the control of an infantry 2nd lieutenant who, true to form, was solely preoccupied with having us "count off" repeatedly, to make certain that he hadn't lost any of us in transit. Our need to look out the window, plus our excited comments about the planes, apparently interfered with his count for the third time since leaving the train, so we were given "Attention," which in "cadet-ese" meant to sit, staring straight ahead, without speaking until given, "At ease." Once we arrived at the barracks, the lieutenant's infantry nature insisted on getting quarters "straightened out, ready for a white-glove inspection," which was a way of saying that we must scrub every surface

I sent this postcard of a primary trainer home to my mother, 30 November 1943 (reverse of postcard, opposite).

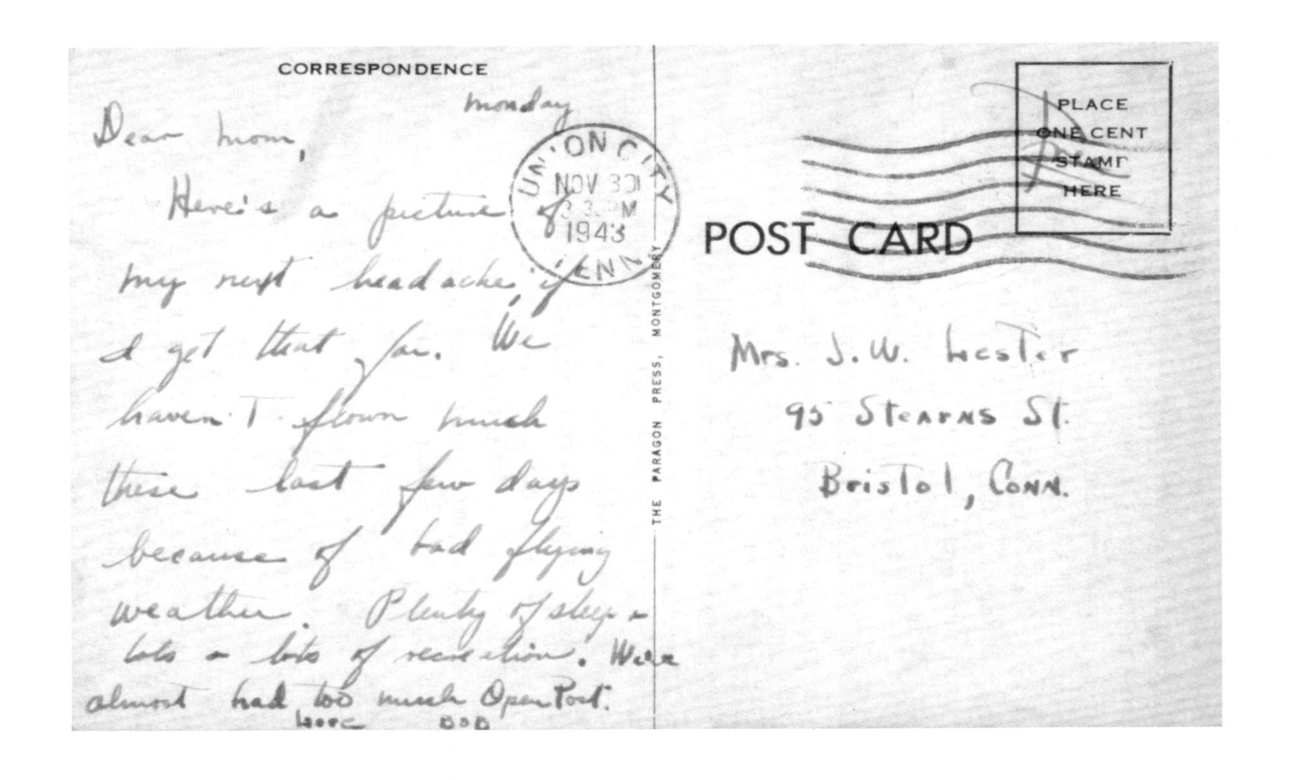

CORRESPONDENCE

Monday

Dear Mom,

Here's a picture of my next headache, if I get that far. We haven't flown much these last few days because of bad flying weather. Plenty of sleep – lots – lots of recreation. We've almost had too much Open Post.

Love Bob

UNION CITY NOV 30 3:30 PM 1943 TENN

THE PARAGON PRESS, MONTGOMERY

POST CARD

PLACE ONE CENT STAMP HERE

Mrs. J. W. Hester
95 Stearns St.
Bristol, Conn.

until it gleamed. Although aircraft were virtually within reach, we spent the first dozen hours on hands and knees, scrubbing and polishing floors.

Two whole days went by while we played at being "Army" soldiers, which in this context meant doing housekeeping chores. We had about decided that we were as far from flight as we had ever been, when on the afternoon of the third day we were double-timed to supply and outfitted with leather, sheepskin-lined flying clothes, boots, gloves, helmet, and goggles. Dressed in these items, we resembled real aviators, just like the image many had carried from childhood after reading of the fighter pilots' exploits in World War I. Some even chose to wear their helmets to bed that night. The goggles were a different matter — protocol demanded that when on the ground the cadet must wear them with the strap around his neck until he soloed. After solo he could wear them on his forehead in the conventional way.

Following breakfast on the fourth day, dressed in our new flight gear, we marched to the flight line. It was a cold, clear, crisp morning with a light frost on every surface, yet the sheepskin-lined leather was almost too warm for comfort.

On the flight line we were alphabetically divided into groups of five, with each group directed to peel off in sequence and report to meet our personal flight instructor. At this point, psychologically, we stepped out of the Army and into the Air Corps, for our instructors, while commissioned officers, also wore wings, which represented the pinnacle of achievement for every cadet. The business of flight immediately captured our total attention as a soft-spoken 1st lieutenant, with a distinctly Southern accent, identified himself and gave "At ease," pointing to the PT-23 behind him.

"Gentlemen, this here's an airplane. That back there is the tail and these big things that stick out on both sides are wings. Up front, that's an engine, and when it works it turns that long thing in front that's called a propeller. This here plane was designed to fly up in the sky, but to do it right it needs a pilot. You all are going to get to be pilots so that these planes don't have to just sit on the ground.

"To learn to fly you got to pay attention to everything I say because the laws of physics operate whether you understand or not. To take to the sky may be the most exciting thing you ever do, but never forget that the air is an unforgiving medium. Done right, flight is thrilling; make a mistake and you can die. We got a job beyond learning to just fly. We have to fly the military way, which means prepare for combat. And we know that a pilot's skill may be the only thing that saves him in a dogfight. If we start out right, you'll find it easier as you move on through training. Study your manuals

Left: Roommate from 37th Street, Chicago, modeling flight gear.

Below: A PT-23 up high.

A typical Air Corps picture: "briefing" poses that drag you from life into the cadet system.

'cause I want you to know the construction and behavior of the -23 as well as you know your best gal. Report to me tomorrow, and we'll see if we can get one of these engines to run and maybe we might try to make one of these things go up in the air. Dismissed."

In all the weeks that followed, our instructor never made another speech that long. Oh, he talked regularly and often, but in staccato comments:

"Switch On! Crank that sonofbitch," to the cadet trying to build up enough crank speed to get the inertial starter to kick over a cold engine.

"Taxi this thing. It don't know where it's going, less you tell it. Use your brakes to turn. Easy on the throttle. We don't want to take off on the flight line. Let's just wait till we get out on the field. Keep making S turns 'cause I know you can't see over the nose from back there. OK. Line her up. Let's see if this thing'll fly. I got her. Off we go into the wild blue yonder!"

On the first flight after being reminded to check my seat belt, "less'n I wanted to practice my parachutin'," there was a dizzy series of many-turn spins, loops, snap rolls, and slow rolls. Looking back over my head to find the earth returning was, until that time, truly the most exciting thing I had ever experienced. The instructor watched my reflection in his mirror for any sign of air sickness. Finding none, he said, "Ya got it," and coached me through my first loop. After a couple more snap rolls, during which he had me follow through on the stick and rudder, he said, "I guess you're not going to be the air-sick type, but if we keep up these aerobatics much longer, I will be. Let's go home. You steer. I'm going to let go of everything. Keep that compass heading. Fly straight and level. Watch your altitude. Constant air speed. Look outside the damn airplane! You can't see where you're going with your head in the cockpit. Use the horizon as a reference. Fly her, boy! Fly her!"

There were classes in the evening, physical ed, and the flight line every day. If we weren't flying, we were cranking the starter for a fellow cadet's plane. Time itself seemed to fly, and always we talked maneuvers, while we flew every imaginable situation with our hands. There was the ever-present talk of check rides fed by the almost daily appearance on the flight line of the squadron commander, who would take a hop with a cadet, only to declare that he was not suited to be a pilot. Following that official declaration, the hapless student would just disappear from our ranks, never to be heard from again. We knew that some, who were not given to air sickness, went on to become navigators and bombardiers; but from our perspective, they had been overtaken by disaster.

After 7½ hours of dual instruction, I was scheduled for another flight, which I expected would involve an hour of practice maneuvers — chandelles, Immelmanns, Cuban eights. In contrast to his manner on previous flights, the instructor said nothing as we taxied out except, "Line her up and take off." I began to wonder. Have I been that bad? Is this my last chance? Maybe even a wash-out ride? Or at least a preliminary to one with the squadron commander?

The takeoff was good — he ought to accept that. In my earphones I heard, "Cadet, take her around the pattern and land, now!"

He sounded unhappy. This was it. The infantry, tomorrow. Well, at least my last landing would be smooth. I lined up, came in, rounded out — too high and bounced it, certainly not the best landing I had ever made. Maybe I didn't belong in this business.

I expected to be directed to head back to park and shut down. Instead he came on with, "Line up for another takeoff." Was I going to get another chance?

Right in the center of the field, the instructor climbed out of the front cockpit, stood on the wing, and leaned over to holler so I could hear over the noise of the engine.

"Cadet, I got me a beautiful wife and two kids. I want to stay alive and that ain't likely to happen if'n I stay in the plane with you driving. I'm gettin' off right now, right here. If you're crazy enough to fly with you, then take this bird off, right now! I'll watch from down here where it's safe."

And he jumped down and pointed in the direction of takeoff. I wasn't quite sure what had happened. What did he mean I wasn't safe? Then I got mad and hit the throttle and was in the air before I realized it. Now there was nothing to do but stay in the traffic pattern and try to land. On the downwind leg I realized for the first time that I was flying all by myself. From then on it was all up to me. If good, I did it. If bad, I did it.

On this landing I touched down light as a feather. My instructor waved me on for a touch-and-go. In the go-around, for the first time I felt the thrill that every pilot experiences when he understands that destiny is exclusively in his hands alone, together with the complete sense of freedom that occurs, whereas while earth-bound mortals are tied to a dull existence in only two dimensions.

As might be predicted, on the third landing I bounced again. Waiting at the flight line, my instructor smiled as he said, "Maybe you can learn how to fly." The guys made a big issue of my right to wear the goggles on my flight helmet where they belonged, especially since I was the first in my group of five to solo.

And thus began a lifetime love of aviation. As Ernest Hemingway similarly noted, nothing is as lovely as a "great airplane."

Kirk

Curly black hair and an infectious smile, never grim, always optimistic, and always just behind the power curve, he would do what we would do. We would escape, but Kirk would invariably get caught.

We met at Primary Flight School in Union City, Tennessee, in 1943. The planes were the PT-23s, with open cockpits and an aerobatic capacity to test the abilities of what we felt were a new breed of fighter pilots. Regulations forbade simulated dogfights, but with so many planes on solo flights, they really couldn't keep track of us all. Kirk, along with the rest of us, wore a long, silk scarf designed to stream in the wind so that we could keep track of each other. As I recall, Kirk wore green; each man had his own distinctive color. The game went like this: wait in the sun until you spotted your quarry, identify him by scarf color, check your six — your rear — and split-S for his. (Relative position bearings were given in terms of a clock, with the pilot seated in the center.) One cloudy afternoon, Kirk flew the above sequence, but forgot to check for the scarf. The maneuver was perfect, but he wound up right on the tail of an instructor, who flew in tight wingman position back to base. This particular instructor could swear better than most, but Kirk never reviewed the dialogue except to say that he was directed to walk 20 tours.

Cadets might get passes some Saturdays and Sundays, if they were ahead on the flight schedule and had no tours to walk, and if the training officers were not too displeased for some real or imagined indiscretion. Consequently, we hardly ever got to town. One snowy day — Christmas, in fact — we were all confined to barracks for somebody's mistake, though I can't recall what or who was involved, if they ever did tell us. Everyone was angry, and we collectively hatched a plot. Somehow we had acquired a collection of detonators, which the paratroops used to rig booby traps. We strategically dispersed them throughout the base, some to explode if a toilet seat was raised, some if it was lowered, some if you lay on a bed, some if you got up from the bed, some if you opened a door, some if you closed it, some instantaneous, and some on timers. Christmas turned into a reasonable facsimile of the 4th of July, especially with the sounds of sirens of both fire and Military Police rushing in all directions.

In the chaos, we walked across the airstrip through an open field to the road to town where we easily caught rides. We realized that we would have to be back for bed check by 2200 — that is, all except Kirk. By the time it occurred to him, it was too late to walk. Instead, he drove up to the front gate in a hastily rented car at 2155. The MPs were less than impressed with his attempt at promptness, and before this escapade was over, he had walked another record number of tours and had to pay double to get the rented car returned; he wasn't allowed any other option.

I was surprised one day to see him sitting on his bunk with his head in his hands. The dialogue went like this. "What's up, Kirk? You look like you've lost your last friend."

"I think I got a dose. If I turn myself in to the flight surgeon for treatment, I won't be able to graduate with the class. I'm going in town to a civilian doctor and not tell the Air Corps."

Penicillin was new and given in multiple shots initially for sexually transmitted diseases. For a week, we watched Kirk at calisthenics suffer with his arms full of needle holes. By the end of the week, he gave up and went to the flight surgeon, only to find out that all he had was "a strained peter."

A week's leave was in the offing, and Kirk spent his time collecting money from all of us. His intention was to buy an expensive fur coat, which he was sure would be sufficient to convince the light of his life to accept his proposal of marriage. He got a loan from everyone, which with interest committed his next six months' pay. He proudly displayed the coat, which cost $4,000 plus, just before his departure. Within three days he was back, as crestfallen as I was ever to see him.

"I got to her house just at twilight. Didn't ring the bell because I really wanted to surprise her. I opened the front door quietly, turned the corner from the hall into the living room, was about to say 'Surprise,' and there she was intimately involved with a sailor on the living room couch. I got so mad I just threw the coat at her and left without saying a word. To top it off, hitchhiking back, I got picked up by a drunken paratrooper who, in the course of the trip, suddenly decided that he should take revenge on the Air Corps, since the previous week a Troop Carrier pilot on a practice mission had dropped eight of his buddies into a lake and had drowned them. He pulled his jump knife and chased me for half a mile."

I still have a copy of the orders authorizing my commission as a 2nd lieutenant in the U.S. Army and my rating as a pilot in the Army Air Corps. Both orders include Kirk's name. We separated after graduation. I'd like to believe his luck held and that his "mistakes as usual" never resulted in more than a temporary, often amusing (for us), inconvenience.

Chapter 4

Basic Flight Training

Newport, Arkansas
January-February 1944

Cadet Detachment Class 44-E,
Newport Army Air Field, AAFTC

Near Miss

Basic was where we began night flying, instruments, and formation in the BT-13 Vultee Vibrator. This basic trainer acquired its name from the sound made as the prop pitch changed and because of its unique stall characteristics. Most aircraft offer kinesthetic sensations as a warning when approaching a stall. Not the BT-13. You sat dumb and happy until it actually occurred. At that point, the bottom just fell out; everything began to shake at once, enough to make your teeth rattle. The stick was useless, as the nose went over to begin a tight spin, which usually required three turns and some altitude for recovery.

All thought and attention turned to mastering this aircraft, together with learning the new skills required. At this point in training, there was but one goal: to get those silver wings. The unacceptable alternatives, getting killed or washed out, were always on our minds. Protocol dictated no discussion of the first, except to analyze the details of an accident so that the same "pilot error" would not recur. Unfortunately, throughout training, there were many examples to study. In fact, statistics indicate that almost as many pilots were lost in training as in actual combat.

After we had initially been accepted for Cadet Training, and in the first formation at Maxwell Field, we were told: "Look at the man on your left, now on your right. One of you will get your wings, one will get killed trying, and one will wash out." This prediction did turn out to be quite accurate, although at the time each believed that he would be the lucky one of the three.

As for washing out, too many friends failed the check ride, disappearing often the same day to a fate seemingly almost worse than death. They were destined to be among the "ground pounders," never again to play with clouds or touch the stars. So we studied constantly to pass the academic hurdles, practiced maneuvers in the air to maintain the level necessary to satisfy demanding instructors, and concentrated on our deportment as cadets. The latter was never quite successful because tac officers, usually without wings, seemed bent on making our lives as miserable as possible. We all were sure that they gave us tours to walk only because they were jealous of our freedom in the sky, while they would be forever earthbound. We were gigged for the lack of shine behind a belt buckle, a speck of dust under the heel of a shoe, or sometimes for disobeying a direct order when one superior demanded attention while another simultaneously demanded name and serial number. The rationale for such treatment was that it would toughen us to withstand pressure, develop frustration tolerance, and teach a panic-proof, cool-headed style. In addition, we also learned what it was like to be on the receiving end of the arbitrary use of authority. It was perhaps for this reason that flying officers rarely experienced difficulty in dealing with enlisted men.

It had been raining at Newport for nearly 24 hours, pouring down steadily — a real toad strangler. The schedule said we were to be at the flight line even though the birds were grounded. We marched in the rain, dressed in the heavy fleece-lined flying clothes needed for the unheated cockpit. The rain continued in sheets so thick that I literally could not see the cadet immediately in the rank in front of me. I followed by watching the water splash from his boots as he walked. In its way, the rain was a blessing, for once ensconced in our squadron operations building, there was nothing we were scheduled to do. Hangar flying began and was interrupted almost immediately by a shout, "Attention." As if by reflex action, all cadets were in the required brace.

Entering my peripheral vision was a small (about 5'8") 2nd lieutenant. He strode in like a bantam rooster, puffed out his chest, and proclaimed: "We got weather, men!" I chuckled. To think they had dispatched a weatherman to help determine what all that water was doing, falling from the sky. I suspect some other cadets may have smiled as well, but I was in the lieutenant's line of vision, and that was it!

I regained composure immediately, but I could see his face redden as he stuck his nose under my chin yelling, "Mister, you're in a brace!" Obviously, he saw no humor in the situation, nor could I expect mercy, for he was within his rights to call me on my indiscretion. In my mind I was already resigned to a stack of tours, probably sufficient to keep me from any time off for at least the next month while I practiced marching with a parachute.

He turned to the group and said, "At ease. All but this cadet." Then he proceeded to drag a chair up to the table in front of me where he sat and began to stare at me. It struck me at that moment that this situation was taking on all the aspects of a senseless contest, but that my future could be at stake.

He had a weapon in his repertoire that was deadly. A cadet could be dismissed for what was termed "Improper Attitude." The presence of this "condition" was strictly a judgment call by the superior and could be based on the fact that the cadet either smiled or frowned while at attention. This was a challenge I had to meet.

At first I decided that this wasn't too bad a deal. He'd play this game for a while, and I could escape any tours. No matter that I was in a brace next to a potbellied stove that was glowing red hot. Certainly a man smart enough to be an Army officer would realize that the fleece-lined leather I wore would be miserably hot next to that stove. Knowing that, he wouldn't keep this up for long. But time passed and he didn't move. The noise of all the others gradually lessened, then all but disappeared. I knew everybody was watching me and wondering how long this was going to last.

While the sweat ran down my arms and legs and dripped off the end of my nose, my Irish temper was going in the opposite direction. I began to consider killing the little bastard, but in a way that would indicate he had won. I decided to be stubborn and try to hold out at least until I passed out. After coming this far, I wanted those wings.

After what seemed an eternity, for I was lightheaded and had lost all track of time, the silence was broken by another "Attention." This brought the lieutenant to attention along with the other cadets. The captain, the squadron commander, and the colonel, the base commander, came into my line of vision.

The colonel looked into what were probably glazed eyes, though I had kept the poker face up until then, and said, "Mister, you are at ease and I want to see you in my office in one hour." He turned to the weather officer and said, "Lieutenant, I want to see you there right now. The rest of you, as you were." And he was gone.

With help, I finally sat down, though my legs didn't seem to want to bend. I could almost pour sweat from the boots, while guys kept bringing me canteen cups of water. One had timed the ordeal at 42 minutes. Another had sneaked out a back door and had gone for help to the squadron CO, or the situation might have lasted even longer. Everybody offered encouragement, but I realized that their approval was no guarantee of my future.

While I took a shower and dressed in Class As, I kept wondering if I would be allowed to continue to wear the prop and wings of a cadet after that incident. I reported on time at the base commander's office and was directed to knock and proceed by a first sergeant, whose stoic facial expression told me nothing.

I took a deep breath, knocked, and entered in response to a crisp, "Enter." Up until that day, I had never been directly addressed on any topic by any officer higher than a major, and that only once. Here was a full-bird colonel who wore the wings of a command pilot. I saluted, reported, last name first, "Present as ordered," and prepared to receive my sentence.

The colonel, sitting at his desk, returned my salute with an "At ease," which in this situation really meant "parade rest," where you stood, feet at 45 degrees, with hands folded behind and looking straight ahead. I couldn't see his face but his voice sounded just great as he said, "Mister, I thought that you would like to know that lieutenant is now a buck private in the Army, who will be digging ditches starting tomorrow. You are dismissed." After keeping my poker expression throughout the proceeding, it was hard to keep from smiling, but I did until I got to the outer office where the first sergeant winked at me.

And so it was over. I had come that close to getting washed out, but as they say, close only counts in horseshoes and hand grenades.

Incidents: Air
Newport, Arkansas

Freedom of the skies, vast caverns of clouds, dreams of unlimited space all became distorted in Basic Flight Training where the possibility of bumping into other planes became a high-priority concern. Using one runway, as many as 100 BT-13 Vultee Valiant trainers and B-15s (variants of the Valiant) would be active at the same time, and in the hands of cadets with less than 100 hours' experience. Radio contact among planes and with the tower was possible but, with so many on the same frequency, was not always too effective. Often the traffic controllers had to resort to green and red Aldus lamp signals. In the event of a declared emergency, red flares rocketing from the tower warned everyone to clear the airspace for the cripple's approach to the runway, sometimes making it instead of crashing.

On clear days, we played an aerial game of musical chairs with 30 planes circling the field pattern at 1,000 feet. The instructors observed their charges through binoculars and would designate a plane by tail number. This was the signal for that cadet to immediately cut the throttle to full idle and make a power-off landing. This game could be a real challenge because the BT didn't behave well as a glider. Of course, the best place to be called was just turning on the base leg and the worst place, past halfway down the runway into the wind. The instructors saw to it that we had chances from every compass point. Here, too, we learned the radio game of "Who dat?" It went like this:

> Instructor: "627, cut power and follow through touch and go, now."
> Cadet (not necessarily 627): "Who say that?"
> Instructor: "Who said that? Get off the air."
> Cadet (now almost anyone): "Who dat that say who dat?"

I've heard this game continue for at least five minutes, and everyone counted the number of "Who dats?" voiced by the last speaker, which made him a minor celebrity for the day at least.

Basic was also where we were introduced to the mysteries of night flying. The airspace around the field was apportioned into sectors, which in turn were allocated several altitudes. Once you become familiar with it, the night sky is almost magical — the stars sparkle and a full moon makes everything soft in silver, especially when the ground is snow covered. But this sense of beauty comes later, for in the beginning everything is strange. The horizon, which had been a dependable reference point, becomes deceptive — *Those lights? Are they on the ground? Stars? Another plane? Am I in the correct sector? At the right altitude? What difference does that make if some other guy gets in the wrong place? And all those panicky voices reporting, "There's somebody in my sector!"*

A BT-13 Vultee Vibrator.

With thoughts like these going through my head, the very first time up at night at what I knew was my sector and altitude, there it was — another plane coming straight at me. From 5,000 feet I split-S, my first aerobatic maneuver at night, to avoid a mid-air. Of course I reported the interloper in my sector. Through the jumble of radio voices, my instructor advised that I had just escaped the reflection of my left wing red passing light as I flew into a cloud puff. For the first time I was scared in the air, but it wasn't to be the last time. This was my introduction to flight that consists of hours of serenity, unexpectedly interrupted by moments of sheer terror.

Here, too, there were night landings, first with the floodlights plus runway lights, plus our own landing lights. Next, without the floodlights, then without floodlights and runway lights, and when the moon was out with no lights at all. For a reason I've never understood, my night landings were always whispering three pointers, hardly a consistent feat for me in the daylight.

Because my night landings were good, I was often assigned to aid the instructors in keeping track of their students who were practicing at night. I had a clipboard, an Aldus hand-held signaling lamp, and the assignment of recording the instructor's rating of each landing. The Aldus lamp was either to green them in or wave them off with red. As usual, there were always many planes in the air at one time, and it was never dull. For example, the running lights of two planes would suddenly appear on approach separated vertically by no more than a few feet, both aiming for the same point to touch down and completely unaware of each other's position. In response to the instructor's frantic radio command, "Top plane on approach, turn to the right," they would both begin to turn, for neither knew whether he was the top or bottom.

The instructor would come back with, "Plane on approach, there are two of you, one above the other. Hold your altitude. Do not land. Proceed straight ahead until you spot the other, report, and await instructions." In the meantime, I gave them the red light. This interlude lasted no more than two minutes during which, in so short a time, two lives and two planes were close to destruction.

And so it was most every night. Little wonder in the rush to turn out pilots that we lost as many in training as in combat.

When God is in his heaven, the earth is underneath, the sky is blue, and you can see the horizon, then "flying by the seat of your pants" works just fine. But in clouds and storms, night and sleet, there is no visible horizon; you can't tell up from down, right from left. Under such unfavorable conditions, birds have the sense to stay on the ground, but people try to fly. And without instrument training, they sometimes kill themselves.

We began by going "under the hood," which was a device for screening out all visual stimuli except the instruments. To the instructor's query, "Can you see?" I replied, "Only instruments."

"That's all you are supposed to see. Ignore your own sensations, and fly those instruments."

I watched the airspeed, the rate of climb, and the altimeter and calculated that we were in a loop and over the top, all three reversed; then because of their lag, I crept toward straight and level. He yelled, "You got it."

My body said we were still in a dive and, after all, the altimeter was still unwinding. Because I had learned that planes don't fly well below sea level, I pulled the nose up, stalled, and the Vultee went into death-rattling shakes, then began to spin. The needle went one way, the ball the other. I wasn't even sure which direction we were turning as the instructor pulled out.

This was my first experience of loss of orientation and control in flight, and it underscored the fact that instinct is not only not enough, but may be even dangerous. We had to learn to trust the gauges. It was this very first experience of a spin on instruments that later contributed to my success when I had to recover a much larger plane as it spun out of a thunderhead.

Chapter 5

Advanced Flight Training

Blytheville, Arkansas
March-June 1944

Squadron C, Class 44-E,
Blytheville Army Air Field, AAFTC

Hot Dog

Day-night cross-country was the last step in Advanced Flight Training before receiving our wings. The flight — from Blytheville, Arkansas, to Jackson, Mississippi. The plane — a Curtiss AT-9 (unofficial name, "The Jeep"). The pilot — with a little over 200 hours — was anxious to do this right, complete training, and be free from cadet restrictions.

The AT-9 was an unusual plane. According to a summary of the plane on display at the USAF Museum,

> The Curtiss AT-9 was designed as a twin-engine pilot transition trainer at a time when there was a need for a "hot" trainer with light bomber landing characteristics. The AT-9 was not easy to fly or land, which made it particularly suitable for teaching new pilots to cope with the demanding flight characteristics of a

new generation of high-performance, multi-engine aircraft such as the Martin B-26 and Lockheed P-38. Stressed metal skin construction. Span: 40 ft. 4 in.; Length: 31 ft. 8 in.; Height; 9 ft. 10 in.; Weight: 6,062 lbs.; Wing loading: 24.78 lbs/sq.ft.; Engines: Two Lycoming R-680-9s of 295 hp. each; cruising speed: 175 mph; Range: 750 miles; Service ceiling: 19,000 feet.

A story had long circulated that the AT-9 had originally been designed, pre-WWII (first flew in 1941), as a Navy night fighter, but that the Navy took a look and threw it back. The all-metal body was said to be "streamlined," which was a popular word of that time commonly applied to trains. It was fast for a flight trainer (maximum 200 mph) and so contoured that airspeed could be reduced 15 mph by simply opening a cockpit wing window just a crack. Its most memorable characteristic was the landing configuration, for with full flaps, the normal approach glide angle made it look like a "streamlined brick." We shared the advanced training base with the AT-10, a much more reasonable design for fledgling instruction. The fact that the -9 landed much faster than the -10 made for frequent, interesting runway situations — but that's another story.

The difference in the two types of aircraft developed the pecking order mode, and those of us who flew the -9 were cocky, believing we were destined to go into combat in planes such as the Lockheed P-38 Lightning fighter, the Douglas Havoc A-20 twin-engine attack bomber, and the Mitchell B-25 and Martin B-26 Marauder medium bombers. At that time, the B-26 got publicity as a plane that, like the bumble-bee, had a wing area too small to fly, but did it anyway. Later I talked to B-26 pilots who had transitioned from the AT-9. It was their opinion that the B-26 would have been an appropriate trainer to have flown before trying to fly the AT-9. The Air Corps apparently eventually arrived at a similar conclusion, for the training class following mine was the last to fly this plane. It was reported that losses in training due to the design of this model far exceeded that of any other advanced trainer.

Suffice it to say, the AT-9 was one of a kind, not well known (only 491 AT-9s and 300 AT-9As were built before production ended in February 1943), and it looked like a "hot" airplane.

With a fellow student as copilot, my cross-country trip to Jackson was uneventful. As we approached the field, we called for landing instructions and received altimeter setting, wind information (20 mph straight down the runway), clearance into the pattern, and the warning that there was a flight of Flying Tiger P-40s in the area.

As a nearly graduated Army Air Corps pilot, I had every intention of making a whisper-soft, perfect landing with the turn to the base leg. From a left approach, I was concentrating on the runway, when my copilot said, "OH, MY GOD, LOOK!" Coming at us from the right were seven P-40s, echelon down, the bottom P-40 at no more than 50 feet. I could think only of getting out of the way of this flying juggernaut. I went to full throttle and lowered the nose, really picking up speed as I crossed the T and began a new downwind leg into the wind. I turned on base and then approached with the wind, dropped full flaps, and came in with tires smoking. We ran the entire length of the runway and still needed brakes to turn off at the very end. They say any landing that you can walk away from is a good one, but I was hardly proud of that one. We taxied to park in front of Operations, and as we shut down, the plane was immediately surrounded by a crowd. All were curious and anxious to view the new, super-fast addition to the Army Air Corps inventory.

We realized that we were being met with adulation, not censure. No one there had seen an AT-9, and they assumed that the hot landing was simply indicative of a very speedy aircraft. With this realization, we more than played the part. Before getting out, we put on our cadet hats with the big silver propeller flanked by the gold wings. This brought an expression of amazement from several, who could not believe that cadets would be allowed to fly such a hot airplane. Collectively, they took it as an indication that the Air Corps was developing faster in sophistication than anyone had imagined. Needless to say, we did nothing to discourage their viewpoint. It would have been a shame to disappoint them with the truth, and we would have had to become less than "hot" pilots.

Incidents: Air

Abe was always congenial and was thought of as an all-around great guy by his fellow cadets. He was especially favored because he was much better than an average pilot, which is why he finished all the requirements for his wings and commission almost two weeks ahead of the rest of the advanced class. Now only waiting for the ceremony, he had nothing to do until graduation. Typical of his nature, he volunteered to ride copilot for his classmates as they finished up.

On one such occasion, Abe was riding the right seat of an AT-9, which

Opposite and left: Curtiss AT-9s — from a manual issued at Advanced Flight Training at the Blytheville, Arkansas, airbase.

WHAT YOU SEE IN THE AIR

was being piloted by an Army 1st lieutenant who, as a student, was in the process of trying to win his wings. As they came in for a landing, the lieutenant had not allowed for sufficient separation from a preceding AT-10, which touched down at a much slower speed than the AT-9. Unless something was done quickly, the -9 would chew the tail of the -10 before it could clear the runway. The tower issued a radio warning and fired a red flare, but the lieutenant froze and held to his approach. Abe waited as long as he could, for there is the rule that only the pilot in command can give control of the plane to the copilot. But this wasn't happening, so Abe took control. He intentionally bounced the plane off the runway and, with full throttle, barely cleared the tail of the taxiing AT-10 as he retracted the landing gear and went around.

Many observed the close call, including some of the brass, who called for convening an accident board, even before the details were known. With time so short before graduation, the proceedings moved fast and the board delivered the following:

The cause of the near accident was due to pilot error on the part of the crew of the AT-9.

The first lieutenant was remanded for retraining in the next upcoming cadet class.

Abe was washed out, having committed the cardinal sin of assuming control of an aircraft without the pilot's permission. It was suggested that Abe be allowed to enroll for training as a navigator or bombardier.

And so the Army Air Corps lost a good pilot, the only Jewish cadet in the class. As for the lieutenant, I'm sure he got through the next class. Don't they say, "Rank has its privileges?"

Chapter 6

Transition

Alliance, Nebraska
July-November 1944

2111th AAF
1st Troop Carrier Command

First Assignment

In my first month of getting used to being 20 years old, the Army Air Corps saw fit to declare me both a gentleman and a commissioned officer, as well as presenting me with a pair of silver wings. So much, so fast, topped off by my first leave in two years.

Two weeks later, back for assignment, I found that the hurry-up-and-wait syndrome had taken over. After hurrying back, I had to wait until the Army could decide what to do with me. In its infinite wisdom, I was assigned to make the world safe for democracy by functioning as a supply officer, at least until they could come up with a plane for me to fly. Having been a Boy Scout, I knew that supply had to do with bunks, blankets, pots, pans, etc. Maybe there was purpose in the assignment — maybe.

I reported bright and early on a Monday morning, uniform creases sharp, new shoes and brass shining. The corporal at the main desk snapped to attention with such precision that I looked around to see who was there before realizing that I was the recipient, in fact, as his new commanding officer.

My response time at Nashville had proved measurably adequate, so without too much delay I tossed off, "As you were," in what I hoped was a casual manner. I must digress to remind the reader that as a cadet, which I had been for the last two years, I stood at attention for everybody, even trees and telephone poles on dark nights, and officially spoke only three phrases to other uniformed personnel: "Yes, Sir," "No, Sir," "No excuse, Sir."

But back to my command. The corporal showed me to my office, offered to bring coffee, and added that the master sergeant in charge would be along any moment to meet with me. His reference, by tone alone, indicated that in his judgment this sergeant knew the score. I retreated to my office to await his arrival.

Ten minutes later there was a sharp rap on the door, and in response to my "Yes?" there appeared a genuine prewar trooper, a Regular. In addition to the six rockers up and down indicating master sergeant, his lower sleeve was covered with length-of-service chevrons that indicated he had spent more years in the service than I had lived! He was 5'9" with a wrestler's build, cauliflower ears, and a ruddy face that looked like a map of Ireland. He had a Brooklyn accent, and in both mood and manner he appeared confident and emotive, a streetwise, sassy Irishman. After the formalities, which really were casual, he launched into a monologue clearly designed to get this "shavetail" off on the right foot.

"Lieutenant, the first thing you have to learn to get along in this man's Army is you gotta look busy. You don't have to really work. You just have to know how to make it appear that you're always busy. Get a big manila envelope and stuff some paper in it and leave it on your desk. You should keep your office door closed so you can read funny books, nap, whatever. If someone knocks on the door, take the envelope in hand before you open the door. If it is someone you want to see, OK. If not, you tell them you are late for an important meeting, and because you are carrying that envelope, they would never suspect otherwise. What's more, they will decide right there that you are a fast burner, going somewhere in this lash up."

In my two-week tour as supply officer, I gleaned much from this crusty old-timer. For example, in response to the warning that we should anticipate an IG (Inspector General) inspection, I poured over records to find that we could not account for 900 blankets. I turned to Sarge with, "What are we going to do about this?"

He winked, picked up the phone, and dialed Operations to say, "Give me the tail numbers on the last two planes that crashed."

Bob Lester, 1944.

"There you are, lieutenant. We lost 500 blankets on one plane and 400 on the other."

I wondered aloud how that could be when both were training planes that wouldn't actually have room for more than 20 blankets if stuffed in every conceivable place.

His reply, "No problem, supply pukes don't know one plane from another; after all, they are all infantry types."

At the beginning of my second week, I was asked to meet with the Military Police to discuss what they termed a "very sensitive matter." It seemed that someone had broken into one of our unused recreation rooms, and the finding of stained tissue suggested to them the possibility of homosexual activity. An MP lieutenant and six men were searching every inch of the building as I stood off in a corner, certain that I could no more be a policeman than I could be a real supply officer. As they went about their sleuthing, they stirred up considerable dust. I idly watched the dust motes in the air as they flew through shafts of sunlight to finally settle on a netless ping-pong table. There, etched in the dust, was a form that to me certainly looked very female. I motioned to the MP lieutenant and simply pointed to my discovery. He announced, "Investigation concluded."

Toward the end of my two-week career as a supply officer, the IG, a full-bird colonel, did inspect. Upon completion, he asked to meet with me and my 1st sergeant in my office. We walked in to report to him, for he was sitting behind my desk. Following salutes and formal presentations, he gave us "At ease, rest."

"Lieutenant, Sergeant, you have a discrepancy. There is a .50-caliber machine-gun, brand new, still in Cosmoline, and it's not indicated on any forms. Detail two men to dig a hole and bury it. Once that is done, you will have a perfect record, and I intend to record the results of the inspection as outstanding in compliance with excellent management skills. Congratulations."

My Irish mentor had the gun buried and then dug up and replaced on the shelf within the day, for inspectors general move on quickly to other assignments. In the process, he observed that this experience simply confirmed the fact that supply people didn't understand the Air Corps. Otherwise the colonel would have realized that there were only training planes on this base, none of which carried guns. He'd gotten this gun from a supply sergeant on another base; eventually it would trade for a case of the best Scotch!

It probably is true that God invented whiskey to keep the Irish from taking over the world.

Paratroops

George Field
Lawrenceville, Illinois

Combat Command, which specialized in hauling personnel, equipment, and supplies, was formed about the same time as the Curtiss Commando C-46 came on line, and this Command built a reputation flying the Hump. Troop Carrier was a different breed of cat, for while during the war we did haul everything imaginable, our primary purpose was to put paratroopers and gliders into combat behind enemy lines.

Initially, using Douglas C-47 Cargo Skytrains, we participated in the training of the 501st, 502nd, and 503rd Paratroop Battalions, which were the foundation of what was later to become the 11th, 82nd, and 101st Airborne Divisions.

To this day, I continue to marvel at the thought of those men who were casual about the prospects of a night drop behind enemy lines, weighed down with over 100 pounds of equipment. On landing, with the use of hand-held crickets (clickers), they had to assemble almost immediately to defend themselves, for it took at least three men to make contact and get a gun up and firing. If the drop zone was under attack, they tossed grenades and fired Thompson submachine-guns as they floated down. While I came to know paratroopers on the ground and watched them leave my plane, I can only imagine what it was like on a drop zone, because we stayed above it all.

On the ground there was a certain swagger, based on the confidence that they had met the requirements of tests in jump school. At the time, these were our first specialists — hand-picked volunteers, whose exploits became the model for what in later years came to be known as Green Berets, Seals, and Special Forces. Their uniqueness was evidenced by the jump boots and the bloused pants, which provoked an occasional unthinking GI to refer to them as "bloomers." This invariably led to a response from the paratrooper, which usually resulted in a broken limb and/or the unconsciousness of the speaker.

In the air, I was often there for a first jump and, for some, their 100th exit. The procedure was always the same. When the pilot flashed the red light, which was on a panel by the open door, the jump master would shout, "Stand up. Hook up. Check equipment (each man checking the straps of the man in front of him). Stand to the door." When the green light flashed, the jump master would yell, "Go," and push number one and any laggard, for even a short delay could leave a trooper too many yards away from the preceding man. Individuals, squads, and platoons needed to be close together to fight

Douglas C-47 Cargo Skytrain.

effectively.

In the cockpit, our job involved staying in formation, a problem that varied according to one's location in the stack relative to the other planes. The greater the number of ships, the more difficult the problem, particularly if one was on the inside of a turn, where despite the air speed of the lead plane, the inside was always close to a stall. If a stall occurred, the C-47, temporarily out of control, might collide with planes in a lower echelon. The pilot would try to hold air speed at 100 mph as troopers exited. In a large formation, to hold this air speed was a feat in itself, for with planes so close in trail, any variation in the air speed of one aircraft would cause a domino effect. We heard horror stories of planes out of control, flying through descending "sticks" — a line descending from a plane — of troopers from a higher formation.

Finding the drop zone and estimating winds correctly was essential in order to be able to give the jump signal at the appropriate time. An error in the cockpit could leave troopers in trees and in lakes, where they would likely drown because of their heavy equipment. Once I did watch an entire squad drop into a lake and disappear because the pilot had miscalculated

Ford-built Waco Glider.

wind drift.

Training jumps were at 1,000 feet, which gave time to use the emergency chute if necessary. Combat jumps were at 450 feet, with no time to compensate for a streamer, but with less time to invite enemy fire.

For the Pathfinder units in Douglas C-47 Skytrains, locating the drop zone was critical or a whole divisional effort would be futile. Pathfinder had been conceived as the solution to the paratroop losses in Europe: select top crews, train them in pinpoint navigation to approach a target below 50 feet, pop up and drop a stick of eight paratroopers. These men would then set up a radar beacon to which a second Pathfinder plane would lead a wing or more of Troop Carrier planes.

In training, three percent casualties were expected due to failed chutes and sprained or broken ankles. In combat, casualties often were much higher before the outfit could even get in a position to fight back. However, once organized on the ground, the sky troops were second to none in combat effectiveness.

Paratroopers have always been proud, and with reason. To be a "Screaming Eagle" is not for the squeamish.

Glider

The first time on takeoff, when you gave full throttle in the C-47 while towing a CG-4A glider full of troops, you'd wonder if you'd make it before you ran out of runway. The procedure usually turned out to be a "piece of cake," but that's because the CG-4 was a medium glider, and it became airborne well before the C-47 did. Before the C-47 left the runway, the towed glider was airborne and in the hands of a pilot just as was the tow plane. With the two ships tied together, problems in flight control occurred only if the pilot of the glider lost control, for example, diving unexpectedly and thus putting the tow plane in a stall. Either pilot could always cut the glider loose if the situation warranted.

Despite the unjustified misgivings about the first takeoff when pulling a glider, the whole set of doubts returned the very first time you tried taking off with two in tow. Your well being depended in part on the skills of the two tail-end "Charlies," who, as long as they stayed attached, could only go where you took them. In Troop Carrier, we quickly learned the routine: launch, reach the objective, signal the glider to drop off, return to the base. The only test of our flying skill involved the ability to drop the tow line for recovery exactly in the center of a target circle.

The Waco cargo glider, model 4A, was large enough to carry a fully equipped infantry squad or a jeep, mortars, light howitzers, etc. Two in trail, fully packed, constituted a considerable load, which required some attention in the cockpit of the tow plane, because it also had to keep position in formation. Leading a group or wing formation towing gliders, as we later did in the Pathfinder units, required the highest level of skill, because we had to consider such factors as the stall speed of planes on the inside of turns. If as leader we were too slow, the inside planes would have to cut their gliders loose to regain flight control. In the meantime, those on the outside of the turn had to increase speed to stay in place. The larger the formation, the more the turning speed plus current air turbulence became critical variables, which required an accurate judgment by the pilot of the lead ship.

Finally comfortable with our roles, we developed misgivings all over again when directed to take off towing a British Horsa glider, which had a wing span nearly the size of our tow plane and was designed to carry a whole infantry platoon. The Horsa was a monster — as big as a C-47. The Brits towed it with their four-engine Halifax bombers. We learned to pull it with our two-engines, but it always felt as though we were dragging a barn door.

Excitement appeared when we began to practice ground snatches of the CG-4A. There would sit the glider with its tow cable attached to a harness suspended between two poles some 20 feet high. We would come in low enough so that our tail hook would snag the suspended cable. On contact, we would immediately acquire the weight and drag of the glider, which demanded full throttle as we reached for altitude. It was a matter of pride that we not have to go around for a second try. The idea of the snatch was to be able to recover the glider for another mission. Until this technique was perfected, gliders were considered expendable, to be used only for one mission. The concept of expendability was evidenced by the fact that glider pilots actually practiced landing on fields studded with poles, so that they learned to intentionally shed their wings, while hopefully preserving the fuselage with themselves and passengers intact. These pilots expected that on landing they would grab a weapon and become part of an infantry unit, usually right in the center of a battle. Proportionately, their casualty rate was very high. I feel that those who wore silver wings with a "G" on the shield were never given sufficient recognition, sandwiched as they were between Army Air Corps power pilots and the infantry.

When I met my first instructor glider pilot, who was charged with familiarizing us power pilots with the CG-4A, he was already famous for two things. As a flight officer he had just returned from the China, Burma, India (CBI) theater where he had flown in the Myitkyina invasion, our most successful aerial incursion up to that time. His second basis for fame was that he had just recently been divorced from Betty Grable, who was the number one pin-up girl of American males, in and out of uniform. Jackie Coogan had been a successful actor before the war. He continued afterwards, as well, with the role of Uncle Fester in *The Addams Family*.

My first glider flight was with Flight Officer Coogan as instructor. I can still recall sitting at the edge of the runway as the tow plane began to move, watching the tow rope playing out. And then we were flying, though the tow plane had not yet left the ground. There was a steady hum from the vibrating connect cable, so different from the engine sound to which I had become accustomed in the air. Other than keeping the wings level and staying above the tow plane out of his prop wash, there was time to survey the surroundings. The absence of power controls and the customary flight instruments took some getting used to. Over the drop zone, Jackie cut us loose. I saw the tow cable go speeding away, still swinging from the tail of the C-47.

Immediately, I was sailing in a silence so complete that it was awe-inspiring. There was only the slightest whisper of the wind, and a sense of graceful lightness made it seem as though I could float forever. Jackie just smiled, for apparently he understood that all power pilots have a similar reaction when they fly for the first time without the ever-present noise of an engine. I'm sure that the feeling I experienced explains the popular appeal of soaring. And it is interesting to observe that now a fast jet outruns its own noise! Suffice it to say that the heavens were meant to be quiet.

Landing the glider is an exercise in judgment. Floating as you do when cut loose, you spiral down, trading altitude for a decent landing approach to touchdown. Although you don't come down that fast, what you give in altitude, you can't have back. In the parlance of power pilots, every landing is "dead stick." Once committed, there is no changing your mind.

This also applies to flight when you are sitting in the glider for a snatch and grab. Nothing. Then the roar of the tow plane passing overhead, so close that you could reach up and touch it as the bulk entirely fills your windshield, and suddenly your air-speed indicator goes from zero to 100 mph in seconds.

So it was that flying with glider pilots gave us a sense of what it was like to fill their shoes on the flying side of the ledger, but they also won our admiration for their willingness to become foot soldiers after descending into the thick of battle.

Airdrome Officer

Lieutenants regularly were given the chance to prove their "command skills" by assignment to manage the flying operations. Flight officers, being appointed rather than commissioned, were not eligible for this duty. Higher ranking officers always had more important things to do. The duty came regularly, and with time it was tolerable once you grew accustomed to it. One learned to know the line chief, the right people in the squadrons, maintenance, the motor pool, the Military Police, the crash crews, medical people, and even chaplains. Officially the airdrome officer (AO) had the authority over flight operations equivalent to that of the base commander, but knowledge of the internal "hands-on" power figures was necessary to get anything done correctly. In summary, if the sergeants considered the AO to be a decent officer, things went smoothly. If not, nothing seemed to work quite right.

On one particularly memorable day, we had received a distress call from a C-47. The weather was down to minimums, and I was in process of closing the field to traffic. The aircraft was on single engine, weighted down by clear icing, low on fuel, and requesting landing instructions. Obviously, there was nothing else for the pilot to do but try to get in, even though it had begun to sleet with visibility less than an eighth of a mile. He was almost a third of the way down the runway and slightly off to the side when he could see the lights. He made a desperate attempt to get back on center line, a feat that would have been possible on two engines, for the C-47 is perhaps the most forgiving plane ever built. However, he didn't quite make it with the one engine. One wheel was on the runway, the other on the soft ground to the side. The plane flipped as one gear collapsed, and continued sliding upside down off the end of the runway.

I jumped into a jeep and raced the crash trucks out to the site. It was raining hard, but there was no other sound. The odor of aviation fuel — avgas — was pronounced, yet so far there was no fire. The nose had crumpled and broken open, exposing the two dead pilots, hanging upside down from their still secure seat belts. The fuselage had been twisted and smashed almost flat toward the tail. The crash crew, made up entirely of civilian employees, just stayed in their vehicles and played their searchlights on the wreck. I asked the chief what the hell was going on and received the answer that they were afraid of fire. Besides, they could see that the pilots were dead. I had no information as to other crew members, because the ship was not from this field; but most C-47s carried a crew chief on every flight, sometimes a radio man and navigator, and often passengers. I ordered the chief to direct his men to do their jobs. He just looked at me as an MP lieutenant drove up in

"In the control tower" — from a manual issued at Advanced Flight Training at the Blytheville, Arkansas, airbase.

tandem with an ambulance, sirens screaming. I directed the lieutenant to arrest the chief, to run off all the civilians, and to replace them on the vehicles with the military line personnel who had begun to show up.

I thought that others might be trapped inside and decided to find out for myself. The door was off, and taking a flashlight I crawled toward the tail in what became an increasingly confined space. I could see or hear nothing and could still smell the gas. It was time to back out, but I was stuck. I yelled for someone to get a grip on my feet and pull. While I waited, I thought of fire. After what seemed an eternity, a buck sergeant with wings etched on his fatigues grabbed my ankles and pulled me out. Instead of staying scared, I got angry. Visitors began arriving, driving down the runway to view the wreck. I directed the MPs to arrest anyone who approached this spot without my permission, and I added, “No exceptions!”

We got the bodies out — there were only the two pilots — and sent them off in the ambulance. We cleared the runway, but not before a few captains, majors, and one lieutenant colonel were escorted off the field. Back at Operations, I called the chaplain and sent him to the hospital with the information regarding religion gleaned from the dog tags. I contacted the aircraft’s home base with a report of the accident. I arranged for a guard on the wreck and made a survey of the runway to assess its suitability for flight the next morning. With the report written, the incident, which had begun at twilight, was concluded in time for breakfast at the Officer’s Club. The base commanding officer approached as I was about to take my first bite of food. With a smile, he said that this was the first time he had ever been threatened with arrest, and on his own field at that.

His next comment was, “Well done.”

There was also an incident when a request for emergency landing instructions came from a P-51 Mustang. In response to the controller’s “Say Emergency” were the words, “I’m having a baby.”

It was for such situations as this that the Air Corps in its wisdom had airdrome officers. The controller promptly dumped the matter in my lap.

I knew that planes even as hot as the P-51 were flown by female ferry pilots, and this was definitely a feminine voice. Women have babies. Therefore, we should take her at her word.

I cleared all traffic for emergency landing of the Mustang and directed an ambulance to the end of the landing roll. The pilot was transported directly to the hospital, delivered a baby boy on the way, and ended up with her husband, who was stationed on the base. Just in the nick of time, a happy family of three became united, thanks, at least in part, to air power.

Another time, during my assignment as airdrome officer, two students were in an AT-10 and could not get the gear down. Their instructor took over in the tower and directed them to attempt to dislodge the gear by abrupt pull-ups. The thought was that the G-force might be sufficient to unstick the wheels. After they had made several unsuccessful attempts to lower the gear, he directed them to ascend to 4,000 feet and bail out. By the sound of the voice in response, this was not a welcome idea.

After reaching the assigned altitude, the pilot made what appeared to be one last desperate attempt to shake the gear loose, only to stall and go into a spin. There should have been sufficient altitude to recover, but the two were inexperienced and scared. They tried bailing out, both striking the tail surface. One chute opened fully, the other was a streamer. The plane crashed and burned. As AO, I had to dispatch personnel to three different points of contact simultaneously.

I headed for the point where the open chute had come down in the midst of a plowed field. At first I could see nothing. Then a blob of white caught my eye, apparently the parachute; it was moving. It seemed to me that there was no way the pilot would be inclined to move that fast and away from our jeep. There was the passing thought that he might have a head injury and was disoriented as we raced across the field. We caught up quickly only to find a local citizen trying to run away with government property. In a not-too-friendly fashion, I asked where he had found it. We followed the pointing finger and found the body. There was a head injury, but it had happened when he had hit the horizontal stabilizer.

Another time, a plan was implemented to move an entire Troop Carrier Wing, gliders included, from Alliance, Nebraska, to George Field, Lawrenceville, Illinois. As AO, I had to formally sign to clear this move. Though still a 2nd lieutenant, by that time I'd had some experience both towing and flying gliders.

Normally the Wing would have made the move without incident. That day, however, there was a line of storms bisecting the route from northern Canada to southern Texas. I consulted with the weather office, which reported that things wouldn't get better, just worse. I refused to clear the move.

Within minutes I was at attention in front of the brigadier general who commanded the Wing. He wondered what a pipsqueak 2nd looey was doing ignoring his orders. I stuck to my position, stating that I didn't believe that tow planes could get through that weather. He let go with a blast, a magnitude that I hadn't experienced since being a cadet. I reminded him that he could relieve me of the position of airdrome officer if he so chose. He did.

All planes took off as scheduled, and the storm scattered gliders and aircraft from Canada to Texas. It took us three weeks to collect the strays, and there were casualties — the numbers became a military secret. Stories abounded of tow ropes breaking, tow planes stalling out, and gliders coming down with poor visibility and few instruments. Not one Horsa made it that day. There was even the story that some citizens throughout the Midwest thought they were being invaded as CG-4As and Horsas glided silently into their midst.

I never saw that general again, for he wasn't there when we finally got things sorted out in Lawrenceville. You can imagine the stories about what happened to him.

There was also the time as I was sitting at a desk in Operations when the door burst open and in strode a corporal in fatigues, right past me and toward the office door of the Operations officer, who was a major. Obviously, the corporal was in a hurry, but there is such a thing as protocol. And it was the job of the AO to see to that on the flight line. So I said, "Wait a minute, soldier. Where do you think you're going?"

He paused, pulled back his collar, and before my eyes he turned into a full bird Colonel, saying, "CID [*Criminal Investigation Division*]. I'm here to arrest that son of a bitch." And he did, for it seems that the Ops officer had been selling gas on the black market, pumping only a part of each truckload into the field tanks and selling the rest outside the base. The colonel had been posing as a truck driver for three months in order to collect evidence.

Once, only a buck sergeant and I were manning Operations in a snowstorm. Clearly there would be no flying, but the routines continued regardless. Some orders came through for a squadron down the line. I suggested that the sergeant wear my heavy leather flight jacket against the blowing snow. Minutes later more orders appeared. I decided to deliver them myself, since it was only next door and Operations wouldn't be left uncovered for long. I grabbed the sergeant's jacket, stepped into the foyer next door, scaled the envelope at the flight officer sitting behind the desk, and turned to leave.

His voice boomed, "Just a minute soldier! How long have you been in the service?"

It had been long enough to know that his question was the prelude to getting chewed out. Then I realized that he was seeing a sergeant, since I had no hat. In the back of the room, three master sergeants were sitting by a potbellied stove, smiling like cats that had swallowed canaries. I decided to play along for their benefit.

I scratched my head and asked, "What year is it?"

The FO puffed up with, "Stand at attention. Don't you address your superiors as Sir?"

I answered, "Yes, I do that."

He screamed, "Insubordination! I'll have those stripes."

I said, "OK." I took the jacket off and threw it in his face.

When he came out from under its cover, he was looking at the bar on my collar, and his face went white.

I mentioned that he'd only had that rank for a few weeks and he'd better give some thought as to how to exercise it.

Later the three sergeants came in to say, "Thanks a lot, Lieutenant. That kid needed that."

There was a time, as AO on one of the southern islands of Japan — I believe it was Kyushu — that I had to prepare for an oncoming typhoon. I had already been in three major ones farther south, and I had come to respect their power. I ordered all planes parked so that the control surfaces would be facing the prevailing wind. Preparations completed, we sat back to await the onslaught of what is one of the more powerful forces on this planet.

A colonel, newly arrived from the States, came charging into Operations to inform this dumb 1st lieutenant that parking the planes as I had would destroy all control surfaces. I protested, but I was ordered to turn them around and to see that the wing tips were secured to 6x6 trucks.

We got the job done before the storm hit. I stood beside the colonel and watched many of the C-46s try to fly, trucks and all, as the winds hit 130 mph. I have photos of wrecked aircraft that stretched for over a mile along the parking ramp upside down with trucks sitting on their bellies. Admittedly, many planes still had intact control surfaces.

We never saw that colonel again, but his stay overseas set a record for a short tour.

For the airdrome officer, there was always *something.*

Rosie

Rosie was already a legend when I first met him in 1944, a former airline chief pilot with 20,000-plus hours in the air. He was the guy who flew the experimental model of the DC-3, the plane called Dakota by the British, C-47 by the Army Air Corps, and Gooney Bird by everyone.

As a 2nd lieutenant just out of flight training, I was assigned to the newly formed Pathfinder unit composed of ten hand-picked crews at Troop Carrier Command, Pope Field, North Carolina. All first pilots were captains recruited directly from the airlines. Copilots and navigators had just gradu-

These two trucks were used to tie the planes down in the typhoon. The wind turned the ship over and set the fire truck on top.

After the typhoon — the tie-down trucks didn't help. This was a ship I used to fly quite often.

A couple of liaison ships, after the wind hit.

Another of our trucks “riding high” after the typhoon.

A truck sits atop the belly of the aircraft after the typhoon.

Our mess hall was destroyed in the typhoon.

ated. Crew chiefs and radio men were all master sergeants with ten plus years of experience. To tell the story of this outfit, the first use of radar, and the newly developed tactics for assault would be a story in itself, but this is about Rosie.

On a day when the weather was just fine, I got the assignment as the Pope Field airdrome officer, which usually involved standing behind some air traffic controllers, experienced sergeants, who knew what they were doing. The only concern of the moment was the report that we would probably be visited by a one-star general who was coming to congratulate us on our safety record. Because he was supposed to present an award, it was likely there would be smiles all around.

Three of the Pathfinder aircraft were up getting some flying time. We could listen to their ship-to-ship transmissions, full of confidence and good-humored kidding, as they commented on each other's flying skills. These were the professionals' professionals, with Rosie as the acknowledged leader. He had established the edges of the envelope for the DC-3 (the C-47) and handled the plane accordingly. He would loop, roll, and spin it as though he were flying a fighter. His favorite approach was on his back with a split-S into the approach, air speed above redline, to kiss down at exactly 70 mph, using only the trim tab.

Things suddenly became all quiet and businesslike with the command, "Attention," as the base commander, a full bird colonel, entered, followed by a brigadier general. After an "As you were," we listened to them discuss a new device, which the general had placed on the taxi ramp to measure taxi speeds. It was understood that the speed should never exceed 15 mph to avoid risks to both personnel and other parked planes.

Their conversation was interrupted by a crisp radio request: "Pathfinders, five miles out, request clearance for straight-in approach."

Knowing that the approach would hardly be routine and certain that the brass might not appreciate an air show, I directed the controller to deny permission. With that, the radio came to life with, "You get a little power and you turn chicken shit. Just because you're airdrome officer today, you're trying to dominate the world. I formally repeat request for a three-ship straight-in approach."

Fearing for my buddies, I said, "Sergeant, deny permission."

When they heard this message, all three tried to respond at once. Something about, "altitude sickness, because I'd been in the tower too long; maybe I was drinking while on duty; maybe it was what I'd had for lunch or just plain lackanookee."

Before I could respond, the general tapped me on the shoulder and said, "Lieutenant, grant permission!"

In response to, "Permission for straight-in approach granted," there came the reply, "You really are a good guy after all, so we'll give you a flying exhibition, just for your benefit."

I started to reach for the microphone, when the general said, "Lieutenant, let them come in without any further comment."

"Pathfinders on approach, one-half mile out," prompted the general and colonel to scan the sky in that direction, but they were looking up. I knew better, I looked down to watch three C-47s, their wings overlapping by two feet, their props, virtually cutting the grass as they went by at least 20 mph above the redline. About three miles beyond the end of the runway, two large trees stood with enough distance between to allow for the passage of two transports, line abreast, but not three. As the formation crossed the end of the runway, Rosie came on with a terse, "You guys, better get your heads out." The two wingmen flipped up on knife edge, and all three passed between the trees into trail for Rosie's split-S approach, masterful as usual.

The colonel was white; the general was red. In fact, he looked like he was going to have a stroke. He began to sputter and stammer about, "Crazy hot dogs, courts-martial, breaking rocks for the rest of the war." His demeanor didn't improve when the gauge on his taxi measure read 65 mph as the three planes, their tails in the air, went down the line of parked transports.

"Lieutenant, I want those three pilots to report to me immediately in Operations as soon as they park those planes."

The colonel looked as though he didn't have the strength to get down the stairs as he followed the general, who continued to rave. I turned to watch the three pull abreast in front of the tower and cut their engines. Rosie came on with, "Well, Bob, how did you like that for an air show?"

I answered with, "I was impressed, but there was a general who wasn't, and he wants to see you guys in Operations right away."

Rosie's response was, "Oh, shit," the most common verbal reaction of any pilot who realizes that he has screwed up unequivocally.

I watched the trio climb out and proceed toward Operations as one might observe someone going to an execution. They walked slowly, and I ran fast to get there before they arrived. The general was still red-faced and pacing, but by then his speech was intelligible.

"They'll all be buck privates digging ditches for the rest of the war. That will be after they get out of prison for reckless endangerment of government property and personnel. Hell, they were taxiing at 65, and at 67 they would be flying with their wheels on the ground."

The door opened, revealing a chagrined captain. The colonel was backed into a corner, still white-faced. The general turned to level what was certain to be the biggest one-star explosion that I had ever witnessed. It began, "Captain!" — halted, and changed to, "Rosie!" Wherein the general grabbed Rosie in a bear hug.

That was it. It was all over with nothing more said about the "air show." The general, the colonel, and the three captains left immediately for the

Officer's Club. I wasn't off duty for another two hours, but as soon as I could, I caught up with the group, where they were still hangar flying.

Why had it all come out all right?

Rosie had been the flight instructor designated to give the general his wash-out check ride when the general was a faltering cadet back in the 1930s. Rosie had decided that with some personal attention, he could teach him to fly. He did.

Wings are worth a lot.

Incidents: Air
Fayetteville, North Carolina
December 1944-January 1945

Pathfinder Training
Pope Field

As part of our Pathfinder training, we were hedge-hopping — really a routine procedure, for we were authorized to fly below 50 feet. It was a sunny day, which created some interesting thermals — rising columns of warm air that make flying pretty bumpy. We were on the third leg of a precision navigation mission that required crossing a designated point at an exact time. We'd hit the first two targets right on the second, and we were feeling pretty cocky. I was flying while the captain, a former airline chief pilot in his late thirties, appeared to be taking a little nap.

I had just taken a cup of coffee from the crew chief, when two unexpected things happened at once. The captain, who was only pretending to sleep, reached out and cut an engine. At that moment we hit a thermal, and the coffee splashed up to cover my sunglasses. So at 50 feet I had to go into a single-engine procedure, blind.

The captain did open one eye as we went through the top of a tree with the comment, "Just want to see if you're on the ball." Clearly, he hadn't figured on the coffee, but his comment when we got back and found part of the tree in the right engine nacelle was, "It's just a little piece."

Incidents: Ground

There was a time when someone high up in the chain of command decided that those of us who graced the skies above should learn infantry skills. Consequently, on a misty cold day, the ten crews of the recently formed Pathfinder unit were loaded into trucks and driven to a "campsite," where we were directed to pitch pup tents. As a former Boy Scout, I knew how and I had to help many get started. In the process, I learned new and colorful ways to cuss as my peers contributed their versions. All had developed fixed opinions regarding the ridiculous nature of this enterprise. The project was under the direction of an infantry major, who introduced himself to us in the context of informing us that we were going to learn how "real soldiers" lived.

Then it began to rain — hard. We were soaked through and crawled into the tents in that condition to spend a miserable night. The major got into his jeep and went back to the air base.

Some with forethought had brought Scotch to sustain us, and as the rain came down, schemes were proposed to "get that chicken shit, infantry son of a bitch." The most benign suggestion involved simple murder.

The morning dawned with low broken scud as the rain finally gave up. We were greeted at reveille by the major, all spit and polish, knife creases in his uniform, rested and clearly eager for a day in the wilds. He detached three crews to return to the base with orders to make a belly drop for our edification before lunch. His point was that we should learn what it was like to be supplied from the air and what better way to do that than to be present on the drop zone. We all knew about belly containers, weight 600 pounds, six of which we could carry and drop single or in salvo. The major knew about belly packs only from what he had read in the field manual.

Through the rest of the morning he lectured on this and that, while we tried to stay awake, short-changed on sleep as we were from the night before. I got the radio to talk in the flight for the demonstration. He sat in the jeep in the center of the drop zone, while we judiciously were way off to the side. I informed the captain leading the flight of three C-47s of the major's location and added that these "students" with their feet on the ground had decided to offer a reward of a bottle of Scotch to whichever pilot hit the major with a belly pack.

The conversation between planes indicated that we had piqued their interest and awakened their competitive streak. As they approached, there was an offer to double the bet, pitting one plane against another. This was countered by the thought that they should strike as a group and salvo so that he couldn't escape — then all take credit and split the Scotch.

The major, oblivious to all this, sat in the center of the field, master of all he surveyed, until the formation cleared a clump of trees, dropped to 20 feet, wings overlapping, speed above redline, and let go with 18 600-pound belly packs.

At the last minute, the major perceived his predicament and dove under the jeep as the missiles came hurtling down. Three packs hit the jeep, and the others fell around in a neat circle — testimony to the skill of all three pilots.

The major survived, but he was really shook up. He seemed to have run out of things to say. He decided that we should call it a day. At that moment, we all became happy campers and agreed that all three pilots deserved to share the reward for rescuing us from the life of an infantryman.

Prodigal Son

"Get flying time" was the directive. Take the plane and go places. Committed as we were to following orders, each member of the crew came up with suggestions as to *where* we should go. Because the C-47 had an impressive range, as a first step on a map of the continental United States, Sy, our navigator, transcribed a circle with a radius of 1,500 miles from Lawrenceville, Illinois. Thus, multiple options were obtained, and we all contributed to the list of priorities. Obviously we couldn't go everywhere at once, so we settled for a plan that fixed a destination paired with an alternate hundreds of miles away, often in an entirely different direction. The tactic allowed a choice of two priority cities and increased the chance that the weather, which might close one air base, would be clear at the alternate — really the purpose of one. For that period, a review of our flight plans would show that we visited most of the major cities within a thousand miles of southern Illinois. A city might qualify either because none of us had been there before or because one of us had happy memories of a previous visit. There really was not so much a method in the choices as there was the mystique by which a closely knit air crew just naturally performed as a single entity with everyone working to the same end.

Thus, there was the time when we filed a flight plan for Atlanta, Georgia, with Pittsburgh, Pennsylvania, as an alternate. Somewhere over Tennessee, we ran into an impressive storm front, which was spawning thunderheads up to 50,000 feet. Because this was just a rehearsal for combat and not the real thing, we had no incentive to see if we could make it through to Atlanta. And so without debate, we decided to favor Pittsburgh with our presence. We landed about twilight, and after acknowledging the tower's parking instructions, we shut down, caught a cab, and headed for downtown.

Our plan was to get rooms in the best hotel, spend the night, and take off at 1300 hours the next day. Note how wisely we allowed for some sleep after what promised to be a night "out on the town."

After showers and in newly pressed uniforms that had survived the trip unwrinkled, thanks to our B-4 bags, we met in the bar to plan our evening's odyssey. Certainly, there would be some drinks, dinner, and some more drinks. But just where? In addition, we had to efficiently contend with the needs of the civilians to take care of us both as a group and individually. We would barely sit down at a table before drinks began arriving, courtesy of the management or from some benefactor, who would give us a wave or a salute from across the room. It seemed that everyone wanted to do something for us, and all at the same time. This treatment was not unique to Pittsburgh, but rather something that we experienced in all of the cities that we visited. Why then was this trip memorable?

The answer: Sy! Here I have to digress and tell you something about our navigator, a 2nd lieutenant and a bachelor in his early twenties. He had graduated top in his class and was assigned to our Pathfinder crew whose missions depended on pinpoint navigation. In the air he was the best, and on the ground he was spectacular as a musician.

Wheresoever he went, Sy carried his trumpet; and when he played, he immediately became a Pied Piper. We would enter a club, and in minutes Sy would approach the band leader on the first break and ask if he could join in for a number. We would watch the leader's face as he listened to the request, and even from a distance it was possible to see the skepticism as he undoubtedly considered Sy just an amateur with an inflated impression of his ability. Nonetheless, this was an Air Corps officer, and in our country at that time, military personnel were given every courtesy and freedom.

Following the break, all of the band members would eye him with misgivings as they began the first number. They soon realized that Sy belonged on a stage. In retrospect, it didn't hurt that he was just under six foot tall with a face and manner somewhere between young versions of Paul Newman and Robert Redford with a shock of hair that touched his right eyebrow when he played. He would seem to lounge as the music began, holding his horn as though he wasn't sure what he was supposed to do with it. At that point I'm sure some band members assumed that his being on stage was just a gag. Air Corps officers were famous for stunts; anything to get a laugh. Then the band would reach the point for a trumpet solo. Up went the horn, and with eyes closed, Sy caught the audience and held them for as long as he performed. His rendition of Harry James's "You Made Me Love You" would cause the dancers to stop, push toward the stage, and concentrate on the music — a behavior that only the outstanding band soloists of the time could expect.

In Pittsburgh, Sy was up to his usual form, and as was often the case, he stayed with the band after the club closed at 0200 for a private jam session. The rest of us went to bed.

The next day at 1400 out on the flight line Sy appeared, breathless and obviously in need of sleep. He'd asked his cab to wait while he pleaded his case to stay another day. According to him, he had found the woman he was going to marry. He just couldn't up and leave her. We had to understand that his entire future depended on our agreement to delay until tomorrow.

Gus, master sergeant, 35-year-old Regular Army radio man from West by God Virginia, opined that the city of Pittsburgh probably deserved the uplift that we could provide by staying another 24 hours, what with them having to deal with the war and all.

At this point Goof, our 30-something Regular Army crew chief and master sergeant, observed that the right engine was running a little rough so maybe he'd better pull a cylinder head and take a look. Sy caught his cab back to town, and Goof removed one cylinder head and placed it on the ground under the right engine. Then we all went back to town.

After naps, we all met again in the lounge, anxious to hear the details of Sy's conquest. He seemed a little vague, but did say that he definitely intended to meet with her after she got off the night shift at 0600 the next morning. He intended to spend the evening with the band and then meet her after the jam session. We passed another pleasant evening presumably uplifting the morale of the populace.

The next morning Sy was nowhere to be found. Goof suggested that rust might have formed on that cylinder head, which was left out in the open all night. If necessary, it could take another whole day to get that engine running right. The captain decided that Goof's suggestion should be our fallback position only if we couldn't find Sy. He and Goof went back to the field, while Gus and I stayed to search for Sy. Of course he wasn't in his room, but we checked again. No one from the band was in the hotel at that time of the morning. I decided to try to talk to the clerk at the admissions desk in hopes that I could get a phone number of someone in the band who might be able to tell me where my navigator was.

Just as I was beginning my request, Sy appeared, escorted by two Military Police along with a primly dressed gentleman, obviously the hotel manager. One MP carried Sy's horn in his left hand, while he supported Sy with his right. The other MP held an empty Scotch bottle in addition to helping prop up Sy. The subject of our concentrated attention was "smashed." He tried to smile as he offered me an explanation, which sounded like, "I couldn't find my love and I was just sleeping."

I asked what the charges were. The MP in a sort of hesitant fashion answered, "Sir, we found him sleeping in one of the halls."

Puzzled by the answer, I asked, "Why would you arrest him for that?"

The manager interjected, "He was sleeping on a hotel mattress which he had dragged out of the room into the hall, and he is drunk."

Sy revived enough to add, "I didn't put it there. It was there when I fell over it, so I was just resting. I couldn't find her. Went down in the basement and up on the roof." Then turning to the manager he pointed an unsteady finger and said, "Where do you hide your hotel phone operators? She had such a beautiful voice, and last night she promised to meet me this morning. She sounded like the girl I intend to marry. Where are you hiding her?"

With that he lapsed into what was akin to a stupor, clearly having lost all interest in the proceedings.

This situation required some finesse. I looked the manager in the eye and asked, "What do you know about the China, Burma, India theater of war?" As I hoped, he stared blankly while I continued, "Look at this officer's wings. That sphere in the center represents a globe of the world. You are face to face with a navigator from the Army Air Corps. Without him planes couldn't fly the Hump without crashing into mountain peaks. China would be without supplies. The Flying Tigers wouldn't exist. Without men like this, we could lose the war. I know he looks bad now. He's been without sleep. The strain of his job can at times be unbearable — you could be looking at a case of combat fatigue."

It was a wonderful speech, and if Sy had been sober, he would have taken his horn and blown "Charge."

As it was, the MPs wondered how a man in Sy's condition could have gotten that mattress out in the hall, especially since it wasn't even on the same floor as his room. The manager admitted that there were reports of other mattresses moved into the halls during some current convention revelry.

In my most serious manner, I asked that any charges be dropped so that I could take this brave flier to the air base where I intended to put him on my plane, which coincidentally was fitted out for transporting wounded.

On my promise that we would leave right away, everyone agreed.

Now to fill in the gaps! After the first night's performance, Sy had tried to make a long distance call to a girlfriend, but without success. In the process he fell in love with the voice of the hotel telephone operator. She offered to meet him the next morning when she got off work, if he would pick her up at her station. She neglected to tell him where her station was located in the building. At 0200 there weren't many people around to ask. And then, of course, he had hardly slept for 48 hours, had had too much Scotch, and had a very unclear idea of the location of his dream girl. First he tried the basement, then decided to try the roof, sustaining his search with a swig from the bottle, which he had brought along to celebrate with his "fiancée." He couldn't explain why he never tried the elevator, but had instead walked. He'd made it to the tenth floor before he found the mattress in the hall, and believing that to be an act of providence, he sat down with his horn and the bottle to consider his next move.

Of course, all the details came out some time later, for we didn't hear a word from Sy after we loaded him into the cab and then onto a stretcher in the plane.

I called for taxi clearance for takeoff, and the tower came back, "Army 1234 [*I don't remember the actual numbers, but it was always the last four digits of the plane's serial number*], say your designation again."

"Roger, this is Army 1234, requesting taxi instructions. Over."

"Army 1234, you are listed as missing and probably down. There has been a search operation in effect for over 24 hours. Where have you been?"

"Tower, this is Army 1234. If you will look out to your left to just a few hundred feet. We are that real pretty C-47 that has been sitting here for two days. Over."

We got our taxi and takeoff instructions and headed out. One more time on this day we were to hear from Sy. As we passed over Columbus, Ohio, I called in to confirm our presence in their airspace. Columbus came back with the question, "Army 1234. Is that a hospital plane?"

Before I could respond, a shaky, slurred voice answered, "It might as well be!" Sy had recovered long enough to respond through the microphone that was situated over his stretcher.

Columbus came back with, "Army 1234, say again, you're breaking up."

"Columbus, this is Army 1234, on a routine flight to George Field. We have no patients on board. Over and out."

When we got home, the Operations officer was so glad he didn't really have a lost plane that he was ready to accept the fact that Pittsburgh had slipped up in reporting on our delay situation, which was true. Obviously, he would not have appreciated the real reason for the delay.

So both Sy and Army "1234," were welcomed back to the fold, just as was the prodigal son.

Chapter 7

Marriage: Get to the Church on Time?

We were now part of the 1st Troop Carrier Command, initially at Alliance, Nebraska, and then at George Field, Illinois, where we jumped paratroopers, towed gliders, and practiced formation from June 1944 through December 1944. Repeatedly, we were reminded that we would be shipping out any day, and for a long time I believed it. Then came new orders, assigning me to the 812th Army Air Forces Base Unit, Pathfinder Squadron, Pope Field, Fort Bragg, North Carolina, effective 1 January 1945. Obviously, this could only mean that I would not be going overseas immediately, which again energized my dream and desire for marriage. A glimpse of the situation might best be understood by reviewing excerpts from my letters home.

Postmark: January 3, 1945, Fort Bragg, North Carolina

Dear Mom,

Through some mixup due to changing stations they failed to

pay me your allotment this month, but I have it fixed now and they will add it to next month so in addition to your $225, which will start coming directly I'll get this which I can send you. It really will make no difference for I can send you the $200 and still have plenty since there's no place to spend money except for food and shows, which only cost 15 cents. This is one of the largest posts in the world, over 50 square miles with a population of over 100 thousand, which makes it a self contained city. Fayetteville amounts to nothing at all but since we'll be working all the time, it doesn't make much difference.

The quarters are two to a room, steam heated and very comfortable and the food is better than at the last place. We have plenty of time to sleep, so I'm really pretty well off. The sergeant says that the CO always asks for a 15 day delay after we finish and every class so far of which there have been four of ten crews each has gotten leaves of at least 10 days.

Which brings up a big question. After I left Bert or perhaps as I was leaving her, I definitely decided that on my last furlough we should get married. I fully realize all the objections and the shortness of the whole thing — the uncertain future — the chance she's taking, especially if something happens to me. All these I've explained to her and as I see it she is the one who is taking the big chance, for I can always make out some way if I get back. This GI Bill of Rights even provides an education and support of a family. Of course she might have to work and all this she knows, but she says it doesn't make any difference.

From my point of view I think it's hardly necessary to say I'd like the idea of having a pretty wife waiting for me and perhaps even a kid with my name. You said yourself if you really are in love nothing else matters — and I'm sure I am and I have every reason to believe that she is. This is no spur of the moment idea either — I've been thinking about it ever since we became engaged six months ago. I thought that would satisfy me, but it doesn't because it goes pretty deep.

Sure it's unusual, but so's War. Maybe we are young, but I honestly believe that I'm not incapable of taking care of a family. Under normal conditions I might be, but the Army has a way of making you older and capable of decisions at a lot younger age than if you were living in normal times. If it wasn't the war it might have been something else to prevent it — but that's life —

you can't stop living just because some guy on the other side wants to fight.

I intended to write Mrs. Dube first, but I've always trusted your decisions and never been wrong yet. I think you may see my point of view quicker and perhaps even go to bat for me. You understand, I want you to go over this letter with Mrs. Dube and then you both can do your darndest to try to point out to Bert all the bad points of marrying so early. If you can convince her, OK — that's for me, for I want her to realize what she's asking for. In all fairness I think you should leave the final decision up to her after you have explained the whole story. I don't want to go against either you or Mrs. Dube's wishes and I believe that if you find Bert is still sincere after you've voiced your objections, you'll give us a break.

I think she has had test enough for after six months even though I wasn't there to do anything about it, she's been pretty darn true and I know she's had plenty of other chances to be otherwise. I'm satisfied.

Awaiting an answer, but please not until you've talked it all over with her and Mrs Dube.

It's late and I have classes in the morning, so I'll close now. Happy New Year, even if it's a little late.

Love,
Bob

At that time, war or not, parental consent to a marriage for a boy 20 and a girl 18 was still the norm. Note the reference to money and the concern with ability to support a family — all residuals of the Depression. The letters continue.

Postmark: 14 January 1945, Fort Bragg, North Carolina

Dear Mom,

I know you must think I'm lost, but I've been flying everyday and every other night.

I needn't tell you how pleased I am that everything seems to be working out as I wanted. It seems as far as I'm concerned it's going to be easy to get married since Bert says that all I have to do is get a blood test and be there of course. All the plans and preparations are the part that scare me anyway. I trust you and Mrs. Dube to pull it off in grand style. I expect to be able to bring home almost $500 when I come — my regular pay plus the amount you didn't get last time. Rather you'll get $225 of that direct and I'll bring home the balance, if we leave late — if not I'll get a partial payment and the rest at Bare [*Baer*].

On the insurance I can make Bert and you both joint beneficiaries. Of course, it's figured on your age so you would get much more than she. She'd get a widow's pension plus six months pay regardless of any amount of insurance. As to how much we'll save and who'll keep it etc. we'll hash it all out when I get home. Don't worry, you won't be caught short. I can't change any papers anyway till after I go back to Bare [*sic*].

I can stay at Bare [*sic*] anywhere from 3 hours to 3 months, but I've a hunch it will be about two weeks and as far as I can find out there's no restriction so Bert can come out there for that time until I leave.

I'm not sure when I'll be home. I've told Bert all I know about that.

I hope I can get Bill for a best man, Another officer would look well — especially a flyer.

You and Bert can probably come to some agreement on the money before I get home anyway. So when I get home I'll expect to find everything laid out and waiting.

I don't know anything about it. I've never gotten married before. Give Bert what she wants, since you only get married once and they tell me it means a lot to a woman.

Frankly, all this ceremony scares me to death. I'd rather fly on a single engine than walk down the aisle of that church. Marriage is all right, but why do you have to go through so much to get into it? I guess it won't kill me though. Dad went through it. I'll bet he didn't like it either, did he?

The only reason that I have time to write is because the weather is keeping us down.

Let me know how things are going.

Love,
Bob

PS. Foot locker arrived.

There was parental approval, and to this point a wedding certainly seemed to be in the offing. Bill was a Scouting buddy, a former next-door neighbor as we grew up, and now a fighter pilot in training at a nearby base. He put in for leave in order to be available on Wednesday, 4 February, the planned wedding date. Bare — Baer — referred to the next air base at Fort Wayne, Indiana.

Postmark: 22 January 1945, Fort Bragg, North Carolina

Dear Mom,

I've had two letters from you since my last one. Things have changed considerably since then as you know. Now I can only plan that on the basis of the order which they received, I should be given a leave within a week after I arrive at Bare [*sic*] on the 30th. I'll know nothing definitely of course till I get there. I'll wire as soon as I receive anything certain of course.

I've got my heart set on that church wedding which looks so good in yours and Bert's letters. I know it will be a disappointment to Bert if it doesn't happen that way. There is a slight possibility that I won't get home at all, but I hardly think so and I believe it would be best to go on planning and that it may be moved up a few days.

It seems to me I detect in your last letters some trace of a defense for the rights and especially the powers of womanhood in general. You're suppose to be on my side and warn me against them not cheer them on.

Nevertheless, don't worry. If I have anything to say about it you'll get your grandchild and it will be a girl. The boy comes next. Whatsmore, I intend and I don't think Bert will mind to call her Sharon Elizabeth. I bet you didn't think I had any ideas on it at all.

Postal savings does sound like a good bet. We'll thrash the money question out when I get home.

I guess I'll manage to get through the ceremony OK, but I think a briefing could take the place of the dry run just as well. All the same perhaps we should weed out the crying women, since Bert may feel that they all thought that they had something when they were married and then found out that they had been gypped and that she's making the same mistake.

I can't write Bill until I'm certain about everything. I'm sure he'll use his car, if he can be there.

We've been flying, weather good or bad and will definitely leave for Bare the 30th.

I don't imagine I'll faint, since I never have yet and I doubt if my hair will be too short for I'll be lucky if I have time to get it cut. I haven't even had time to shave for the past three days.

Before I leave Bare I'll know whether it will be advisable for me to come back with Bert, since they may not have me come back till they are ready for me to ship out.

I'm glad to know it will be all right for Bert to have a child and just between you and me I think she might welcome a conspiracy to get one. I haven't much time to read any books so with what I know already plus what you can tell me I imagine I'll manage pretty well. You'd be surprised I think to know how much your younger generation knows about it already. You could even write some more advice in letters and if the censor reads it, it's probably something he should know anyway. If we work it out right we ought to make you a grandmother in no time.

Waiting for your letters and I promise to let you know as soon as I know anything definite.

Love,
Bob

The best laid plans of mice and men!

We finished training at Pope Field on 30 January and were put on "Emergency Alert" — Top Secret, for immediate overseas shipment as critically needed Pathfinder crews; outside contact with the civilian world prohibited.

With just five days to the wedding date, I couldn't talk to my bride. Calls from home to Pope Field were answered with the comment, "The officer is no longer stationed at this base." Bert continued with the plan for the wedding on 4 February in hopes I might still be able to make it.

Back at Fort Wayne, Indiana, the port of embarkation, I was told that a phone call would be a violation of national security, as knowledge of my whereabouts could lead an enemy agent to speculate on the location and possibility of aerial invasions. It had never occurred to me that I could be that important to anyone except possibly to the woman that this arrangement was preventing me from contacting. As regards Bert's significance for me, that can be inferred from my poem to her.

Need I say I love you,
Can't you see it far
Beyond the vast oceans
To the brightest star?

How to say I love you
Can my heart keep pace
To the blue in your eyes
The sweetness of your face?

Heaven is a dream
To which men look constantly.
Here in you I have it,
Unworthy though I be.

The flashing in your bright eyes,
The glorious lights in your hair,
God with his perfection
Has managed to ensnare.

Many men I pity,
For never will they know
The warmth of your embrace,
The love that you bestow.

Long I spend in dreaming
And often stand in awe
How a woman could be fashioned
Without a single flaw.

That God will grant me power
Often do I pray,
That each second, I may love more deeply
Till my dying day.

And He in all His power,
Who has given me so much
May my life even in eternity
Be blessed by your touch.

Little words so foolish
How pitiful they can be.
Darling, I do love you.
Certainly, you must see!

JRL, *ca.* 1944

Fortunately, three of the captains in this Pathfinder group had clout, all recently detached as chief pilots from major airlines. In fact, more than one Army Air Forces general owed his wings to the patience of one of these captains, who in the years past had been their flight instructor when they were still cadets. Collectively, these captains took pity on me and cashed in some chits. On 4 February they came back to the barracks with my orders for a week's leave, plus permission to call home and tell Bert what had happened. We moved the wedding date to the following Saturday, 7 February.

Since I was now on a roll, I pointed out that all of the crew should be allowed furlough as well, because they would have to wait till I got back before they could ship out. The captain phoned the general, and my proposal was approved, no doubt because the captain was owed some significant favor by the general.

Transport was such that I didn't get home until too late on Friday to transact business at City Hall just like any citizen might, but as a contribution to the war effort, on request, they stayed open until I could get there. Then we went to buy the wedding ring, and we got into an argument impressive enough to lead the jewelry clerk to ask, "Are you sure you two ought to get married?" I can't remember what the fight was about, but I know it was dark and I probably said something stupid after she had called attention to the beautiful full moon. At that point it would have been just like me to have agreed that the moon made it "a great night for bombing."

With the wedding date postponed three days, everyone made last-minute changes. The best-man-to-be had used up his leave time and was scheduled to fly on Saturday. With such short notice, I called the one friend who had not been able to go into the service for medical reasons. He accepted the role with grace and reassured me that he had learned to handle his circumstance as one of the few not in uniform.

While in the sacristy, the priest offered to let me escape through the back door before we went out to the altar. The best man chuckled, and I kept my eyes on the beautiful bride coming down the aisle. Then we were side by side, and it wasn't too bad except I recall the ring felt six inches in diameter and I was sure I'd drop it and we would all be crawling around searching for it. There were smiles as we walked down the aisle, now man and wife. As we exited the church, P-47s in finger-four formation crossed in front of us; the leader reversed with a split-S and pulled up in a victory roll. Bill, too, had made it to the church on time.

Incidents: Ground
Baer Field, Fort Wayne, Indiana
February 1945

After a three-day honeymoon in New York, we came back to Fort Wayne via railroad. I had reserved a room at the Hotel Indiana. We drove up to the entrance, and as I was paying the cabby, a very attractive female threw her arms around my neck and gave me a kiss.

I was perplexed.

Bert looked perturbed.

How would I explain this to a bride of less than two weeks? Even while trying to extricate myself from this woman's arms, I concluded that my "buddies" must have set me up.

My misgivings evaporated when I finally got a look at Doris, the agent of this affectionate greeting, who was the older sister of a high school buddy. Doris had married a pilot, who was waiting to ship out. Her enthusiasm was based on the fact that I was the first familiar face from home that she had seen in months.

Doris and Bert became fast friends and supported each other in the uncertain climate of their husbands' imminent departures.

Two letters to Mom summarize the situation.

> Dear Mom,
>
> Apparently we've been lucky for as yet I'm not certain when I'll leave and every night I've had a pass till 02:00. Over the weekend I got a 36 hour pass from yesterday evening till tonight.
>
> Bert's met all the crew and the rest of the gang and they get along swell.
>
> As soon as we arrived I bumped into Doris S. Remember — Burke's big sister? She married a fellow from Waterbury, who is here waiting to be shipped too. She and Bert spend most of the day sleeping and running around till we get in. I believe Bert will

come back with her in the car after I leave. Still don't have any idea how long that will be but I don't think much longer than a week.

Therefore the only problem is the money. Unless you can wire some I won't have enough if she can stay very much longer. I'm certainly glad she did come for I had a hunch I'd have quite a few evenings.

We all went out with the crew last night and had a big time including Doris and her husband. They sort of adopted the boys.

The Captain got quite a lot of time home since he flew both ways. Sy was waiting for us when we got back and one by one they all drifted in.

There's not much more to tell you except I guess I've got her trained pretty well now. I had to write that because she's reading as I write.

You can write to Bare [*sic*] until I get an APO address and then change. I'll get them all even though it may take some time.

Will write more later.

Love,
Bob

P.S. Don't you believe that part about his having me "well trained"! He's just a dreamer — Bert

Dear Mrs. Lester,

Received the money you wired — thanks a million! I'm not in very great need of it right now, but I imagine it'll come in handy if I stay on a few more days — which is very likely. It's a good thing you had the wire addressed "Mrs. Bertha Dube Lester", otherwise I may not have been able to get it — for I have absolutely no identification in my marriage name.

Everything is going along just fine — so far — Bob has been able to get a pass every night. He has reason to believe his luck will keep up throughout this week, anyway. Here's hoping

Bob's just fine — looking swell — though I think he's getting rather fat. It's becoming, so I don't think I have any reason to fuss about it.

Met all of his crew — and I honestly don't think you can find

Bob and Bert on their wedding day, February 7, 1944.

a better lot of fellows. They'd do anything for each other and they're just swell to me. I've never been treated with such respect in all my life!

Everything's fine so tell mother not to worry and don't you, either. Give everyone my love. Tell them I'll write again in a couple of days.

Love,
Bert

Incidents: Ground
Travis Field, Fairfield, California

I have a vague memory of the train ride from Fort Wayne, Indiana, to Fairfield, California, the aerial port of debarkation. Sy played his horn for the benefit of the various military passengers. We admired the mountain scenery and wondered at the vastness of the country, as the train passed from state to state.

Privately, I wondered if I would ever see this land again. No one talked about not coming home, yet the thought was always in the background, which is probably the only plausible reason for the behavior described below.

Once we arrived at Travis, we were told we could depart for Hawaii any time, as soon as transport became available. Each evening we were to check the bulletin board to learn whether tomorrow would be the day. Thus, with no notice, we were granted 24 additional hours in the States and another chance to sample San Francisco night life.

Within a week we had developed a system — shower and dress at 1700; leave by rental car; three stops, en route to the city, where a drink for each of us would be waiting, for we took pride in arriving at each bar precisely at our specified time. So it was that three bartenders learned the meaning of ETA (estimated time of arrival).

Once across the bridge, we sampled as much as we could. I remember Fisherman's Wharf, the trolleys, a French restaurant, and trying hard to convince Goof that it wasn't possible to throw a glass off the Top of the Mark because of the thickness of the glass windows. His contemplated maneuver was probably more the result of "one too many" than because of his lack of familiarity with the urban world. Why, just a month earlier, Goof had received a message from his Oklahoma home, reporting, "We got a spigot in the house."

While I dealt with Goof, Sy and Gus had commandeered an elevator with the intention of offering transport only to beautiful women. At least twice, their invitation filled the car.

After an evening of revelry, we would get back to Travis by 0400, check the bulletin board, hit the sack, and be ready to go again at 1700.

In all of our escapades, at least one of us had always kept a balance to counter impulsive imprudence. In the episode to be described, our collective defenses against recklessness collapsed completely.

Early in the second week of the above routine, we had spent a typical evening with the plan to terminate our merrymaking at the Chinese Garden. Our choice was based on the fact that Noel Toy, a nationally known stripper, was the featured attraction.

We arrived at the Garden at 2330 and were seated at a table on the second floor. We each ordered a drink. The headwaiter welcomed us with the message that this establishment, as was the case for all other city restaurants, was to be closed promptly at 2400, per a new regulation, which was, as of that night, instituted to protect the city from possible enemy air attack. (During the war, the Japanese did launch one plane against Oregon from a submarine.)

Noel, who was a lovely, willowy brunette with shimmering hair that reached to the floor, was to begin her performance at 2340. Before finding a place at the railing, where from above one could watch her on center stage below, I had the inspiration to order doubles for everyone "for the road."

Noel held us all enthralled until she finished her act at 2355.

Back at the table, which was covered with 50 drinks (for each of the crew had experienced the same inspiration), stood the headwaiter. He informed us that we had but five minutes to consume the lot. With no time to argue, we tried.

I lost count at six B&Bs in the first two minutes, and from that calculation I remember nothing until I woke up in my bunk at Travis the following afternoon.

It isn't just that *I* don't know how we got home or even who drove back across the bridge and the many miles to the base. No one *else* knew either. It was a total crew blackout. Never before nor after that episode, to my knowledge, did any of us ever reach that degree of inebriation. They say God takes care of fools and drunks, and we were both on the night that San Francisco also blacked out.

Chapter 8

Southwest Pacific Area

Incidents: Ground
Hickham Field, Pearl Harbor, Hawaii
February 1945

We were sitting on the patio of the Officer's Club at Hickham Field watching the ships moving both in and out of Pearl Harbor. Rosie, by then an Army Air Corps pilot, informed us that he had also been in the Merchant Marine when he was a youngster. He launched into a monologue about the skill and precision common to those who traverse the seas. None of us had ever sailed in anything larger than a rowboat, so there was nothing to do but listen and learn. In his effort to educate these landlubbers, Rosie called attention to a ship moving up the channel toward us. He identified her as an LST (Landing Ship, Tank). As an attentive student, I noted the number on the bow, 822. Rosie translated the signals from the control tower to the ship, signals sent by a vertical string of balls. He informed us that the LST was being directed to berth just across the channel from us between two other moored ships. As a fitting climax to his lecture, he directed us to observe this docking so that we would understand the true nature of experience in a service that dated back to the beginning of time.

The LST slowed, began a gradual turn to the left, and rammed the stern of the moored ship to its right. It then backed away, almost running down a harbor launch, whose crew appeared about to dive into the water to escape. Warning horns were sounding from several craft as the object of our attention made another run at the dock, this time striking a glancing blow to the ship on the left, then hitting the pier with a force sufficient to produce a noise that we could hear, despite our distance.

All but Rosie wound up rolling on the patio with laughter. We begged for more instruction on naval matters, but without success.

Almost three years later, I stopped in a Tokyo radio station to see Tokyo Mose, a GI disk jockey, who had taken the place of Tokyo Rose. Mose interviewed visitors between records; and on this occasion, he spoke with two sailors who were from the LST 822. I asked if they had been on the ship at Pearl Harbor. They both laughed and said that docking had become famous throughout the Navy. On their way over from the States, the captain had become ill and LST 822 was under the direction of a newly appointed executive officer who had never before docked a ship that size. Rosie never knew what had turned his tribute to the men of the sea into amusement for those who had chosen the air.

A Navy PBY Catalina Flying-Boat

It was hot, 125 degrees in the shade of a canvas overhead, no breeze, and no ice for the Scotch. We were stretched out on canvas cots in shorts and T-shirts, and sweating as if in a Turkish bath. We were a hand-picked, hot-shot, Pathfinder, Troop Carrier crew, which had trained together for over a year.

This was our first day in a combat zone at a "repple depple" (replacement depot) on the island of Biak, northern New Guinea. In the previous 24 hours, we had eaten or been exposed to breakfast four times in succession as we crossed the Pacific from Hickham Field, Hawaii, with stops at Tarawa and Manus, as passengers in a C-54. Because everyone carried a bottle of Scotch, we turned to that after the second breakfast. It was about 1400 hours, and since 1200 we had listened to a broadcast over the Biak base radio, repeated every 15 minutes. "Emergency, PBY crew needed. Report to Operations. Urgent."

Goof, after taking another swig of Scotch, said, "Captain, let's go fly that soma' bitch." Everyone sat up at this suggestion, but before anyone else could speak, Goof added, "I think it's got the same engines as a C-47, and we sure know about those."

Sy opined that it would be a lot cooler up there and besides, "Didn't we come to fight this damn war?"

The captain thought for a moment while he took another swallow and finally said, "Let's get into the war."

We all piled into a jeep and headed for Operations, full of the same certainty and good humor with which we had approached the Top of the Mark and those bars en route from Fairfield during the two weeks we waited for a plane to ship overseas.

At Operations, we had our first contact with Aussies. They received us with big smiles and began immediately to explain their problem. One of their pilots had been shot down some 50 miles northwest of the base and was last seen floating in his raft some three miles off the beach of Japanese-held territory. They had been able to keep P-40s over him in shifts for a couple of hours, but the last covering of planes had to return when no rescue plane appeared. Their desperate call had been for someone to try for a pickup, someone to fly an available PBY.

They were so anxious to get us moving that we hardly had a chance to say anything — so busy were we trying to absorb all the information that came pouring out. In pieces and parts the material came together as we were loaded into jeeps along with parachutes, maps, and a constant monologue on radio frequencies, call signs, weather data, fighter escort, suspected enemy tactics, etc.

Gus, our radio man, in a Southern mountain accent that was unique, complained, "Lieutenant, you'll have to help me with these Aussies, 'cause they don't speak English. I can't tell when they say 'point Aoi,' whether they mean A or I. How am I goin' to talk to them when we get in the air if they can't talk American?"

We pulled up in front of the least decrepit of the three PBYs parked opposite a line of Aussie P-40s. Awaiting our arrival was an Atabrine-yellow major with a medical caduceus on his sweat-soaked shirt collar. He volunteered the information that he would come along in case the downed pilot needed help. We barely nodded a greeting, because for the first time all five of us were close enough to touch a PBY.

With the comment, "I'm not sure the damn thing will even fly," Goof climbed in to investigate.

Sy called attention to the waist guns, informed us he was a crack shot, and proceeded to interest a passing buck sergeant with the lure, "Hey, how would you like to be a hero?" This approach worked, because the sergeant was soon helping Sy load the guns.

Gus checked the radios and assured us that we could at least communicate with the tower, as long as they kept an American there.

We found a form showing that this plane had been on a red X for three weeks — not flyable — just sitting with no effort at repair. Goof yelled for a new battery and along with the captain was up on the wing installing it.

In the meantime, I was trying to make sense out of a cockpit unlike anything I had ever seen before. Connecting the control wheels was a line of panels that signaled instructions to the flight engineer, who sat some distance behind the pilots. This was certainly going to be a new experience, since none of us even knew that such an arrangement existed on an airplane. I searched in vain for a flap handle, finally hollering to the captain that I couldn't find it on that thing.

He responded, "Keep looking. I'll be down in a minute. We've almost got this battery set." A minute later he added, "You can forget the flaps. I just crawled out on the wing, and this plane doesn't have any flaps."

At this point the flight surgeon showed some interest. He leaned forward and said, "You guys are putting me on, right? You've had a lot of time in these things, huh?"

I tried to be reassuring with the statement, "I think we've all seen one take off and land in the movies at least a couple of times."

His face was suddenly white in spite of the Atabrine yellow. He shook his head, checked the straps on his seat-pack parachute, then added a breast-pack chute and went back and strapped himself in, all without another word.

Satisfied that the guns would work, Sy decided that the plane needed a name. He scrounged some paint from a neighboring revetment and proceeded to paint "BERT" on the hull, after my bride of a month and the only woman who was acquainted with everyone on the crew, for the rest were bachelors.

We finally got the engines started and were cleared for taxi. En route to takeoff position, I attempted to test the wing floats, which meant throwing a switch to activate an instruction light to the engineer. Goof cussed over the intercom, "Dumb, damned way to fly an airplane, playing with lights and I can't even see out of the soma' bitch." At that moment, as the floats came down, a jeep passed under the right wing and the driver ducked just in time, more startled than endangered.

All of the flight instruments looked familiar enough, and the engines checked out on run-up. We were cleared to take off, but Goof couldn't find the right switch to retract the floats. Then the intercom went out and we were communicating by hand signals while trying to yell over the sound of the engines. The tower came back with, "PBY, you're cleared number one for takeoff. Expedite. You are holding up P-51 flight and they haven't got the gas to burn."

The floats retracted, and anxious to get out of the fighter's way, the captain poured the coals to her. She lumbered and bumped along, picking up speed slowly, too slowly; for three-quarters of the way down the runway, we were only reading 65 mph on the airspeed indicator. A C-47 needed at least 70 mph to get off, and here we were committed with throttles bent all the way but with what seemed like not enough speed to fly. As the ocean loomed ahead and the Cat bumped along, the captain looked at me and said, "Bob, maybe we've bitten off more than we can chew."

I could only add, "Let's try getting it up; flying's better than swimming."

She came off near the end of the runway while we expected a stall any moment. We were accustomed to climbing at 125 mph, and we couldn't even seem to get this speed straight and level. In addition, there seemed to be something wrong with the trim as we were turning right, then left, then right again. While we were trying to figure this out, our P-40 Aussie escort kept crossing in front, barrel rolling as they passed, further adding to our feeling that we were on the verge of stalling. With throttles nearly wide open, we pushed on without radio contact with our fighters. We finally figured that they were not interested in giving us an air show, but wanted us to understand that they would communicate by hand signals.

Without warning, our blister guns began firing. I had a vision of Zeros diving on our six with their guns winking, for I knew just how they would appear, having been exposed to the war movies from Hollywood! At that point I realized that this was no lark. We could even get killed. But there wasn't much time to think like that, because Gus came forward to say that Sy had decided to test the guns and couldn't warn us with no working intercom. He added that all the other radios were out as well.

The captain asked me to look for the manual under the seat and try to figure out how to make a water landing. I called Goof up for a council and summarized with . . . "too shallow and she'll porpoise and break her tail; too steep and she'll scoop water and sink. If we believe all this, we can't land on water." After consultation we decided to just fly until we skimmed the water, then cut the power and hold the nose up when she settled.

We could see the bay and the yellow raft and had just begun our letdown, when suddenly one of our escorts strafed the raft while others hosed the shore. The flight leader rolled past our nose and pointed, signaling, "Go back."

The return flight was without incident, and with a green light from the tower, the landing as smooth as glass. A Navy PBY crew that had just arrived met us at Operations, and having observed the landing, assumed that we were old hands in the Cat. They thought we were kidding when we confessed that this was our first time, until we began to complain about air-speed, trim, etc. Between fits of laughter, they offered the following facts:

> Although the air speed indicator did say mph, because this was a Navy plane it was calibrated in knots; thus our 65 reading translated to 75 mph, and we were really burning up the sky on full throttle where their 120 knots equaled 138 mph. To add to their amusement, they informed us that because the plane had to maneuver on water, the rudder did not neutralize automatically as on land-based planes. Our zigzag flight, if observed by any Japanese, would have appeared as evasive tactics of the first order.

The flight surgeon listened to the conversation, then shook his head.

"I don't believe a thing that happened today. You guys are all crazy. If you are an example of what's to be coming from the States from now on, the Japs won't have a chance. I'm just getting too old for this, but I admit I've never been more scared or had more fun at the same time in my life."

The Aussies filled us in on the aftermath. The long delay before the rescue was attempted had given the Japs time to kill or capture their buddy and replace him with one of their own as bait. Their plan was to entice a rescue plane to land and thus be exposed to gunfire from emplacements, which they had hidden along the shore. The trick didn't work, because the decoy could not give the correct recognition signal. As thanks for our effort, the Aussie squadron presented us with a case of beer, just cooled from a high-altitude flight, that proved to be an improvement on the Scotch that had helped us to get into this adventure in the first place.

Ironically, after over a year of training together, this one flight was the only time we ever flew in combat as an Army Air Corps crew, and that in a Navy Catalina flying-boat!

Incidents: Ground 375th Troop Carrier Group
Nadzab, Papua, New Guinea
April 1945

In New Guinea we were surrounded by jungle with the temperature always 100 degrees plus in the shade and high humidity guaranteed. Every day between 1400 and 1430 it would start to rain and would last for at least an hour. Daily we rolled our tent sides to catch fresh water in order to shave and bathe.

The only relief from the heat was when we were in the air, and ground personnel would hop a round-robin shuttle to a neighboring field like Lae or Seven Mile at Moresby just to cool off.

This was a new world and a curious mixture of cultures: our GIs, Aussies — their wide-brimmed hats pinned up on one side, lending a rakish air — with a demeanor not unlike our Texans; natives; head-hunters and cannibals — the young spear-carrying males with flaming red hair, which signaled the current search for a mate. All applied themselves to repelling the Japanese, who had struck and stuck at Rabaul, Wewak, and the Owen Stanley Range.

Where there were Aussies, every afternoon things stopped for tea. It wasn't bad, but their beer was better, though we couldn't get used to drinking it warm. Our solution — fill a wing tank with the brew, put it on a P-38, and send it up to 30,000 feet. Once there, the pilot would call the tower with, "Beer ship. Ready for immediate landing clearance." Immediate clearance was always granted — the pattern would be cleared and the beer would be cold when he rolled to a stop, where we gathered with our canteen cups.

A sense of what our world was like, externally and internally, can be inferred from my letter home.

April 6, 1945
Somewhere on New Guinea

Dear Mom,

Just a line to let you know I'm thinking of you even though I haven't written. You see conditions — lighting and mosquitoes — don't permit much time for more than one good letter and I trust that Bert gives you all the news. I try to write her every day as I know you'd want me to and what's more returning letters over here especially hers and yours mean a lot more than food or sleep or anything else for that matter.

Your letters seem to take not quite three weeks to reach me but that was with a traveling APO. Now it's a definite base and they'll come straight without following me all over the Pacific. Air Mail is the only thing to use. I expect to be travelling again for a permanent group this time. When I get there I should be set in one place for some time.

I'm censoring mail once in a while and it really gives you a cross section of America. Bert's probably told you some of the funny things I've found.

Without exception the fact that God is important is certainly evident and the Catholics are predominant here. We have a swell Chaplain, who was in ecstacies over the large attendance at Easter mass. Before he began he said he hadn't sung a high mass in two and a half years and wasn't as good as Sinatra, but he figured that God didn't wear bobby socks anyway.

The little chapel is quite beautiful, a palm covered affair, set in a little valley with high mountains behind. It's open of course, more or less just a roof. The pews are just up-ended 500 lb. bomb tail fins.

I've never seen anything like the way it was Sunday. I didn't realize that religion could be so powerful and real. The congregation overflowed onto the hillsides, so many attended — many non catholics, who thought they ought to do something for Easter. You just couldn't imagine what a picture it was with the sun coming up and the mountains all purple with clouds sitting on the top. Dew on everything sparkled like a million diamonds.

And in the midst of all that beauty you knew there was a war for fighters buzzed off regularly for morning patrol from the air strip a little way down the valley. The big bombers took the air with a roar every few minutes, with a roar in fact that almost drowned out the hymns. It was strange, unless you thought about them, you never heard them, for even a three bomber formation, all twelve engines wide open, didn't seem to compete with Ave Maria.

All around were fellows in pistol belts, some in flying clothes, their helmets in their hands. Negro soldiers with garands and carbines swinging on their backs were kneeling on the hillside with Aussies, who look strangely American, when they take off their big campaign hats. There were even some fighter pilots with engine grease still on their faces, showing white where their goggles had been. They'd just come in time from an early sweep.

The priest gave the best and sincerest sermon I have ever heard (don't tell Fr. Monahan). You see he was one of the boys and he didn't seem as though he were in the pulpit preaching. Instead, he was very personal and friendly, as though he were talking to you, as though he were a guy, who just knew the score. It's hard to describe his text — it sort of sunk and stayed, but I just couldn't attempt to do it justice with a pen.

He said that he had been hearing confessions for a week straight, but that he didn't mind because he used to be a parish priest and he'd been forced to listen to women's confessions. He said that they insist on telling their husbands' sins first and then theirs'.

All in all the sermon said you're lucky that you can fight to preserve Christianity, as well as freedom, but it wasn't heroic or anything like that. You just sort of hitched up your belt and had to admit, when he finished, that you wouldn't want to be any place but here, because it was something that had to be done. In fact he said it would take a block buster to get him away from such a gang as he had. I saw what he meant, when at least ¾s went to communion, which took longer than the mass. He ended the final blessing with, "You guys know the score. Keep your heads out."

There was a lot more which I wouldn't even attempt to write, but it certainly was effective. Honestly, believe it or not, it hit so true that tears were running down the cheeks of at least 60% of a few thousand men. Yes, they were crying openly without being the least bit ashamed, but they weren't feeling sorry for themselves — these were tears of pride. I know it sounds screwy and it's awfully hard to explain. I've always prided myself that I could keep from showing my emotions, no matter what, but there was a lump in my throat and as I saw the dozens of combat ribbons under all those tearful eyes, let me tell you I'm not ashamed to admit it.

Sy, my navigator, is not a catholic, but he's a swell guy and we sort of understand each other on religion and we can discuss it without getting angry. Well anyway, I asked if he wanted to come along since his particular faith had no service. He said he'd get lost standing up and sitting down, but I said it wasn't as complicated as it looked, and besides he could watch everyone else. I noticed later how quiet he was as we walked back to the tent area.

I guess he was thinking about it. I'll bet he goes again next Sunday, even if I don't ask him.

Sy said, "You know, Junior (since I'm the youngest on the crew) your outfit has a way of making it stick. In your church God seems to get more what he deserves. Did you see those natives praying? (some had walked for days through the jungle to attend the Easter mass) Gee, I'm glad I went!"

I don't think that needs any comment from me.

Well I sort of got carried away with this letter I guess, but at least it will give you something to read. Here come the mosquitoes, so I'll crawl under the net and hit the sack.

Write often and take care of Bert for me. Seems you won't have a grandson for sometime now.

My love to Ma Dube. Thinking of you.

Love,
Bob

The above reaffirms the statement "There are no atheists in fox holes."

Monkey Business

He came out of the jungle, just walked up to me, and held out his hand. When this happened, I was sitting in front of my quarters, a 16x16 tent roof with rigid screened sides. A Filipino, standing nearby, sought to interpret the gesture of this new arrival with, "He want to shake hand, be friend. Name, Amo." So I shook hands for the first time with a monkey to begin an exchange, which made Amo part of my world for the time that the group was based in the Philippines.

Amo (Tagalog for monkey) had apparently decided to join the human race, which might be cause to question his judgment. In any event, after we shook hands, he became a companion. He was always around except for an occasional foray into the surrounding jungle, sometimes in search of a mate (he never would say), and sometimes in search of fruit, which he would bring back as a gift. In the tent quarters he would sit on the rafters that supported the center pole and sleep up there at night. He indulged in happy chatter, running beside, as we walked anywhere in the compound or on the beach. In the mess hall, the club, or the plane, he would sit on my shoulder.

Amo got angry and/or excited by only two things. The first always occurred when we went swimming. While he would never go in the ocean by himself, he would go on my back with his arms around my neck. Regularly I would swim out some distance from the shore, and on one occasion I dove under water. At that, he let go. I searched the surface, but no Amo. I had about decided that he had drowned, when he appeared on shore, shaking his fist at me and just raising hell in monkey language. The wonder was that he was able to swim that distance under water. Because we lived on the beach at Tanuan and it was always hot, this little scenario was repeated frequently. He never surfaced while returning to the shore, and always he shook his fist and raised a fuss when he got there.

The other thing that angered Amo happened only twice in all the time he was with me, but it took two incidents before I understood. Routinely he went with me to the Officer's Club, which was only a large, tent-topped, screened-in structure with a bar and a few tables. Amo would sit on the bar and drink a beer along with the gang. He would hold a glass in his paws, sort of prop himself with his tail, and chug-a-lug. I learned to ration the amount, because it took less than a bottle to get him drunk. At that point he would develop a stupid, intoxicated expression, not unlike that of a man who was trying to appear sober. He couldn't walk a straight line, and he often needed his tail to steady himself to keep from falling over. He was in such shape one evening when he suddenly screeched, launched himself off the bar, and headed for a table on the far side of the Club. At this table there was a pilot from our outfit with his guest, a flight nurse. Amo was headed for her, but he had to pass her escort, who held him off long enough for me to grab him by the tail, a feat that would have been impossible if he hadn't been drunk. None of us understood his behavior, for he had never tried to attack anyone before. Nevertheless, to play it safe, from then on I kept him on a leash whenever we went to the Club. He didn't seem to mind the restriction, perhaps because he understood that it occurred only in that setting. Weeks passed and I had about decided to forego this safeguard when Amo went "ape" again, screeching and tugging on the leash as he tried to get to a nurse who had just entered.

Fed up, I took him back to my quarters and tied his leash to a bunk. I decided to return to the Club to seek a clue to explain his behavior. This was the first time I had ever left him alone while still tied up, and he shook his fist and screamed at me as I departed, all the while trying to untie the knotted leash. The flight nurse who had been the target of Amo's attention had been in charge of wounded on my plane in the past and she had come to know Amo well. I went to apologize for the episode, while proclaiming my bewil-

John R. Lester in front of a C-46.

derment at Amo's behavior. Why did he seemingly without reason try to attack someone with whom he had been friendly? The nurse calmly explained that she was in the midst of her menstrual cycle. After that we kept Amo on a leash, at least until "the coast was clear."

Amo's claim to fame was the many months of hours spent flying in the C-46 wherever we went. He would sit on my right shoulder and listen to the radio messages coming through my right earphone. If bored, he would climb down and push buttons on the instrument panel, which automatically changed radio frequencies. During flight he had the run of the plane, and he usually spent a lot of that time asleep. On takeoffs and landings, he was in the cockpit and on my shoulder. Then, he would always point at the runway

The C-46 Curtiss Commando.

Right: In the office of the C-46.

Below: A C-46 being loaded with the help of Philippine locals.

as if to keep me focused on the task at hand. Amo had more flying time than many of the crews in the squadron, and he was the mascot and official good luck charm of the outfit. More than once we held up long enough to get him up in the cockpit before takeoff. It was usual for ships checking in to ask if Amo was ready to go. At such times, he acknowledged by squeaking into the mike, when I tapped him behind his ear.

Amo moved with the outfit to Clark Field on Luzon and later flew countless missions throughout the Philippine archipelago, which was really his homeland. He went to New Guinea, Peleliu, and Okinawa, which was OK as long as we always returned to the Philippines. A problem started when we began to spend more time on Ie Shima and then moved to Iwo Jima. Simply put, it was against regulations to permanently transport animals or birds away from their natural habitat. I had a yellow-crested white cockatoo that came under the same regulation.

I tried all the tricks I could think of to have an exception made for Amo, especially because he had become a symbol of success for the squadron. But we had no luck. The paper shufflers kept telling us that there was a war on, something they were certain of because they all had time to read the *Stars and Stripes.*

I made a trip back to Leyte, by then the backwaters of the conflict, to the very spot where Amo and I had first met. He seemed to know that we had to say "goodbye." He pointed at the water and shook his fist at me. He gave me a hug and ran toward the jungle, with only one glance back over his shoulder before he disappeared in the thick foliage.

Incidents: Air
Leyte, Philippine Islands
May-July 1945

There was a time as we headed into Tacloban that our attention was drawn to a destroyer, because it was doing nothing — just sitting still. Before calling in for landing instructions, I decided to check on this ship for I was curious as to the reason for its inaction. At 2,000 feet we had the answer. About a quarter of a mile off the starboard side of the destroyer, there sat a submerged submarine. The sub seemed to be perched on a white coral shelf, and the water was so clear that we could distinguish the meatball painted on its deck.

On the way up from Morotai, as we approached the Leyte Gulf, we had passed two carrier task forces in tandem heading for this location. It was obvious that the sub had positioned itself just south of Samar with the intent of getting a shot at these carriers. Some quick calculations indicated that the sub hunters would have about two hours before the task force was in range.

In hopes of increasing lead-time, I buzzed the destroyer, and we signaled with the Aldus lamp: "Jap sub, on bottom, your two o'clock, quarter mile."

The Navy came back with, "Hi, Air Corps."

We tried again, this time buzzing both the destroyer and the spot over the sub. The response from the ship was repeated; they seemed to be assuming that we were just being friendly. I climbed back to altitude, contacted Tacloban tower, and described the situation. We then got landing instructions. As we left the area, both the sub and the destroyer were just sitting. In retrospect, we should have realized that the destroyer must have known about the sub.

As we entered the landing pattern, we could see two destroyers leaving the harbor at a high speed like a dog with a bone in its teeth, trailing wakes that indicated top speed. A half hour later, some of the crew claimed they heard distant explosions, which they believed to be depth charges.

Three months later our squadron HQ received a TWX from the Navy with the message, "Jap sub sunk, off Samar. Thanks for the assist!"

Another time, we were transporting what was supposed to be a full load of marine uniforms from Nielson Field, Manila, Philippine Islands, to Zamboanga, Mindanao, Philippine Islands. This was soon after we had secured the area, and the field was in bad shape as a result of the recent fighting. The main runway was so badly cratered that we were forced to use the taxi and parking areas for landings and takeoffs. The limited distance necessitated a short field takeoff, and even then clearing some telephone lines required adept handling. In fact, the ship just ahead of us did hit some wires before he could get his gear up.

For our purposes, in the cockpit we considered this to be just a routine flight, especially as this load was "safe-handed" by a Marine warrant officer. We only had to take it from here to there, and the Marine would take care of the paperwork; at least that was the way it was supposed to happen.

We learned later that while we were busy up front, this Marine had gotten into a conversation with our crew chief. He confided that this was his last assignment before returning home after being in the Southwest Pacific for over two years. Obviously solicitous for his own welfare, he paid careful attention to the planes that had been taking off. He asked the crew chief if they were overloaded, which would account for their barely clearing the

Japanese Occupation currency.

obstructions on takeoff. The crew chief, faced with a chance to bait a ground pounder, proclaimed that our own plane was considerably overweight, about a third again as much as the one ahead of us, which had just snared the telephone wires with its landing gear.

We pulled into position, held the brakes, and went to full throttle, while the crew chief stood behind us watching the gauges as was customary. With both engines winding up in "war emergency," we let go the brakes and were off with some distance to spare. I remember the passing thought that this was almost too easy, considering the load we were carrying.

As Mindoro came into sight, the crew chief came up to inform us that we had "lost" our warrant officer. According to others in the cabin, just as we had throttled up for takeoff, he had jumped out the open door. Apparently, the crew chief's story had convinced him that this was not the plane to be in, if he wanted to live to get home. We laughed about the incident, then promptly forgot it, for once we had unloaded, we took on four guards with submachine-guns and 68 Japanese prisoners, who sat on the floor facing the tail. When we were in the air, I remember asking the guards with the guns to stand with their backs to the cockpit so that if they had to shoot, they wouldn't get the pilots with the first volley.

Three weeks later I was called to the CO's tent to answer a grand theft charge involving the disappearance of 16,000 Marine uniforms. I related the incident of the vanishing warrant officer and swore that I knew nothing of any missing uniforms. While I was proclaiming my innocence, MPs had gone to examine my plane. There they met the crew chief and the radio operator, dressed in Marine attire, distinguishable because the pants pockets were cut differently from the Army issue.

It had always been the practice in Troop Carrier to examine any load for useful items, and the crew often supplemented their personal needs by scrounging. In this case, they had appropriated two uniforms each from one of the cartons. However, they could not account for 15,996 uniforms still missing.

The crew was reprimanded and, as the pilot, I caught hell, too. But even after this incident with the warrant officer, I still trusted Marines — unless they were due to go home.

A B-25 of the Bat Squadron.

Chapter 9

Perchance to Dream

The U.S. took Manila, and for Troop Carrier that meant that lots of stuff had to be brought in quickly to sustain the position and continue the drive to retake all of Luzon. There were bombs, bullets, food, fuel, vehicles, guns, medical supplies, personnel, radio equipment, toilet paper, and an occasional jackass (both actual and human). And on the first departures from Manila to reload for more of nearly everything, we carried to freedom American civilians who had been interned by the Japanese in Mt. Santo Tomas prison. (Over 40 years later, in my role as a clinical psychologist, I took a social history from a patient who, as a small child, was evacuated in a plane from our group, for he remembered the marking, "Frontline Airline." He had been imprisoned with his missionary parents from the time that the Japanese initially took Manila. It really is a small world, for I had the chance to help him once again.)

We would load at Tacloban, Leyte; fly into Nielson Field, Manila, unload; pick up wounded, equipment to be repaired, etc., and repeat the loop. South of Manila there was at least one Japanese division, bloodied, but hardly docile, completely concealed in the extremely dense six- to eight-foot-high "cogan" grass. Our fighters were everywhere, and because we had control of the airspace, our flights back and forth were conducive to sight-seeing, usually from altitude. On one round, as we approached Manila we had a ringside seat at the "circus," when the Circus Group, low and moving fast, passed beneath us and headed for that Japanese division.

The Circus Group was famous in the Pacific for effective ground attack. It flew B-25Ds configured for strafing missions with eight .50-caliber machine-guns in the nose, four in side packages, plus two in the top turret. Squadrons at that time numbered anywhere from 18 to 36 planes; a group consisted of four squadrons. Each squadron in the Circus Group was identified by an animal whose likeness was painted on the nose of the plane. Thus, as we watched, the Lion Squadron, wing tip to wing tip, line abreast, opened up with 500 .50-caliber guns. Grass went down as before a scythe, as did the Japanese hiding there. When the Lions had exhausted ammo, the Tiger Squadron swung into position, followed in sequence by the Bats and Bears. At the time, I doubt that the Japanese were familiar with the *Wizard of Oz*, or the sight of the Circus Group at work would certainly have recalled Dorothy's lament: "Lions and Tigers and Bears. Oh My!" Suffice it to say, that Japanese division ceased to be an effective adversary.

We in Troop Carrier just kept going and coming with no sleep other than the cat naps en route as pilot and copilot spelled each other. I hadn't even seen a bed for over 48 hours, when on a leg back to Manila we hit rough instrument weather. This meant not only turbulence but also lightning flashes, which required that we both stay alert to alternate when a flash temporarily blinded the pilot on instruments at the time. The whole process is fatiguing under the best of circumstances, and the lack of sleep added to the problem.

We got in OK, and I picked up a parachute as I left the plane. Why? I don't know. I'd never done that before or since. And in fact, despite all the paratroopers who have jumped from my plane, I have never even thought of using a chute except as a last resort. I know I was punchy from the lack of sleep, and maybe taking the chute was symbolic of an unconscious need to bail out of the whole situation.

It was dark and a fine misty rain fell as I went stumbling toward where someone said there would be a place to sleep. Then I fell into a hole, or rather a bomb crater. It was a big one, and the top seemed way up there with the sides steep and slippery. Even if I climbed out, I didn't know where I was going anyway, and I didn't much care. The rain was warm, the mud nice and soft, and the parachute made a great pillow; so I went to sleep. I was discovered the next morning and allowed to sleep for a couple more hours before I was brought a cup of coffee along with the message, "Sir, it's time to fly again." I felt fine, but the parachute had not fared as well.

That rest cost me $125, the fine for "damage to government property," but I'm still thankful that I never had to use a parachute for anything other than a pillow.

No Tail

A Japanese Zero, its tail riddled by machine-gun bullets, sat in front of Operations on the airstrip at Zamboanga on the island of Mindanao, Philippines. There was inscribed a line from a popular song of the time: "The monkeys have no tails in Zamboanga."

On another "routine" flight back to Manila, we took on a load of 50-gallon gas drums. The weather was a little questionable, but no more than we usually encountered at that time of year. This was before we were able to depend on much help from ground stations for either weather or any form of traffic control. Sometimes we had navigators, but we really didn't trust them. Dead reckoning was the usual method. Soldiers were just beginning to be trained as load masters and were appearing with their slip sticks (slide rules) to theoretically balance our load. But usually we'd wait until we were in the air. Then if the plane was dragging her tail, we would ask the crew chief to start moving cargo and people forward until it felt right. On this flight there was just myself, a copilot, and the crew chief, but we were over max weight because of the number of gas drums aboard. This didn't require unusual procedures, however, for it only meant using one-quarter flaps, full power with the brakes on, then letting go when the engines wound up — in effect a short field takeoff on a long strip. In contrast to the C-47, the C-46 had the power once in the air, and even when trying to get there. It was just a bitch on the ground, especially in a crosswind.

We were off at about 1500 into what was a gloomy, very dark sky for that time of day. At 2,000 feet, we were on instruments with occasional breaks sometimes above, sometimes below, for a brief glimpse of the sea. As we continued to climb — for we'd have to top 10,000 feet to cross Mindoro — it began to get bumpy and the clouds were laced with streaks and flashes of lightning. At about 9,000 feet, a C-47 suddenly appeared heading south. I called him for a weather report, and he replied that while it was choppy, instruments all the way, he'd made it through from Manila. We kept climbing on his reciprocal course, completely encased in rain; and in less than two minutes, the proverbial shit hit the fan.

We were caught in what we later concluded was wind sheer in what must have been a colossal thunderhead. In seconds we dropped over a thousand feet, and while the altimeter was unwinding to catch up, we shot up with even greater intensity. Hail pounded the plane like the hammers of hell, and lightning flashed with such brightness that we had to take turns covering our eyes till the next flash. The plane pitched and tossed so violently that all the gyro instruments spilled and we were left with only needle, ball, and airspeed indicators. The gas drums broke the moorings and began banging into the sides of the fuselage. In one abrupt toss, we were over on our back and into a spin. Never before had I even heard of a C-46 being in a spin, but here it was and winding up fast.

The crew chief, who was on his knees behind the throttle pedestal, said, "Please, Lieutenant, get us out of this. I don't want to die!"

I didn't like the idea either; and I yelled at the copilot, who seemed frozen, to get both feet on the left rudder with me. We pushed with all our strength, and after what was at least a four-turn spin, she straightened out and we regained control.

Unsure of our exact location and afraid we might hit a mountain after having lost considerable altitude, I headed west to get over ocean. We spotted an Army air base on southern Mindoro, and I called for landing instructions. The tower came back with, "Army transport, this is a bomber base; you are not authorized to land."

I answered, "Army C-46, declaring emergency."

The tower replied, "Say emergency."

Exasperated and exhausted, I said, "The damn plane won't fly and I'm coming in. You'll have to shoot to stop me."

All considered, it was a good landing, and I was able to pull off the runway, but I couldn't taxi after the "Follow Me" jeep. I just shut her down and sat, because my knees wouldn't stop shaking. Only then did I really feel unadulterated fear from the sense of being in the grip of a monstrous force over which for a time I had no control. It was 30 minutes before I could step out to observe the damage. The right wing was twisted 12 inches up and the left wing 6 inches down. The outside fuselage was full of holes and dents where the gas drums had been driven into the sides. The tail looked as though a giant hand had tried to rip it off. We just left the plane for scrap. Even if this was a bomber base, this C-46 would never be able to leave. Within hours we caught a ride home to Tanuan, our base on Leyte. The fear was suppressed. We had a story to tell about the granddaddy of all thunderstorms.

It happened that I bunked in the same tent with the squadron flight surgeon. I didn't know it till much later, but he had observed me on the first night back in a dream and trying to get that plane to pull out of the spin. The next day he grounded me for two weeks, because I'd been flying too much without sufficient rest. Nothing more was ever said to me about the dream, but that was not the end. This physician rotated home months before I did, and he stopped to visit my wife and told her the story.

Thus it was that she understood when I kicked that left rudder with both feet, propelling her right out of bed, as the dream returned on my very first night home as a civilian.

This monkey almost lost his tail in Zamboanga.

Gremlins

No discussion of flight experiences would be complete without mention of "gremlins." Some say that these were invented by pilots of the British Royal Air Force during World War II as a means of explaining occasional, unexpected, mechanical failures that occur in aircraft. The idea of "invented" is testimony to the smugness of humans, who often use the term to imply wisdom instead of admitting that finally they have accidentally discovered some phenomenon, which has always been present. Gremlins are no more inventions than are leprechauns. Albeit while leprechauns may tend to favor the Irish, gremlins have no such ethnic preferences — their habitat and activities are in aircraft. Though not directly mentioned, there was probably a gremlin present when Leonardo da Vinci first designed his flapping-wing aircraft, *circa* late 1400s. Certainly, one was in the air with the Wrights, jumping up and down at various times at both ends of the fuselage, first to get an elevator in the front and then a rudder in the rear of the Wright glider (1902-1903).

To assist the non-flying readers (all of whom have my sympathy), I offer several facts that may contribute to understanding these little folks:

a) Gremlins live only in and around airplanes.
b) They appear to only one individual at a time.
c) If one chooses to appear to more than one on a crew, he/she never looks exactly the same to any two humans, a fact that has contributed to the confusing reports surrounding their existence.
d) Gremlins routinely engage in mischief, but they are not malicious, *i.e.*, though they are often reported as responsible for faulty

warning lights and the temporary malfunctioning of flight gauges, they have never been implicated in an aerial accident investigation, which is always exhaustive.
e) A gremlin usually spends his/her entire existence in one airplane, though the similarity in his/her behavior has led some pilots to conclude that they are being followed by the same gremlin from plane to plane. However, the companion in the new plane was probably merely a first cousin. There is an occasional exception in which a gremlin will follow a pilot rather than a plane. But when this happens, he/she never engages in mischief. (see Fifi, below)
f) Gremlins are usually small enough to sit comfortably on an artificial horizon or an altimeter needle. They seem to prefer the flight instruments, though they have been known to lounge on a pack of cigarettes when it is left just above the instrument panel. I think, when this occurs, it is because they sometimes have an interest, as does the pilot, in what is happening out in front. I once saw one who was at least four inches tall, but more of that later.
g) Gremlins are of two genders, but with an equal-opportunity arrangement in that both sexes have equivalent powers. The females are called Fifinellas.
h) Gremlins don't talk. They communicate by gesture, facial expression, and sometimes body English. They do listen intently to both a pilot's words, when he speaks aloud, and to his thoughts, when he doesn't. There is one exception when it comes to sound: a Fifinella will laugh aloud, like the sound of a tiny, tinkling bell.

So much for my thumbnail sketch, and now to my interpersonal relations with gremlins. I remind the reader that every flier's experiences will be different, for while the problems of flight are similar, every gremlin is a different personality, just as each plane, even within a given type, has its own unique characteristics.

I met my first gremlin, whom I immediately knew was named Chauncy, soon after receiving my wings. He did look something like a leprechaun, with fiery red hair and a bulbous nose almost as red. He didn't really walk, but rather seemed to dance as he moved out along my right wing. But I'm getting ahead of the story.

While at Lawrenceville, Illinois, I had a chance to be helpful and get some air time by volunteering to fly a surplus PT-23 from there to Tulsa,

Oklahoma. It had been well over a year since I'd flown in a primary trainer, and I looked forward to having my face in the wind again, a pleasure a pilot must give up in the cockpit of both fighters and multi-engined craft. This PT-23 had been on the ramp too long without flight, but the line chief assured me that the aircraft would hold together at least as far as Columbia, Missouri, which was the refueling point en route.

I drew helmet and goggles, climbed in, and was off — a piece of cake. Because I had learned to fly this plane first with the constant refrain from the instructor, "Keep your head out of the cockpit! Don't fly the instruments, fly the airplane." I took off without even looking at my airspeed indicator. In fact, I didn't notice that the air speed wasn't registering until I set up my course for Columbia. No big deal — I could do it all by the seat of my pants. And so I sailed happily along, just enjoying the open air. After a time, it struck me that I had no radio, a device I had become accustomed to depending on for navigation in the past year or more. This trip was going to require dead reckoning, and I hadn't been paying close attention to checkpoints. I dug out the maps, found the right sectional, and started looking for familiar features to match ground to map. Nothing looked quite right, so I dropped down along a rail line to read the town name from a water tower. I studied the map to find that place, and I was so intent with my head in the cockpit that I ignored my air speed. The aircraft stalled, and I was in a full-turn spin before I could recover. I really believe that this would not have happened had the air speed been recording, because I would have seen the reading and then would have flown with my head, if not my body. At any rate, I was both scared and angry as I pounded the gauge with a gloved hand and looked accusingly toward the pitot tube, which extended from my right wing.

And there was Chauncy. He waved and went skipping out along the wing toward the pitot tube. He jumped down, straddled it, bent over, and looked in the aperture. He jumped back up on the wing, shrugged his shoulders, and held his arms out, which communicated "nothing doing." Then he snapped his fingers and a full beer stein appeared in his hand. He turned and toasted me, chug-a-lugged the beer, and disappeared. You can bet I paid attention to both checkpoints and the plane's attitude to insure sufficient airspeed from then on to Tulsa. Diagnosis at Columbia — bees had built a nest in the pitot tube.

Another time, we had been up one messy night in a C-47, bucking through clouds of rain and occasional sleet, when the controls began to feel sluggish, almost as though the plane just didn't want to fly. The deicer boots were on, but they weren't doing the job, and we were losing our airfoil's lift. The captain asked me to confirm with a spotlight what we both knew was the case — clear ice — while he tried a lower altitude. In spite of the rain, in the spotlight I could see the boots pulsing on the leading edge of the wing, yet the clear ice had formed leaving an airspace at that point. The wing itself was covered with a clear ice sheen, on which a gremlin, in a racing stance with his hands behind his back, was skating. As the plane lost altitude, snow appeared; then the ice began to rime (become crusty) and start to break off in chunks, taking the skater with it. I reported the observed change in the effectiveness of the deicer boots, but said nothing about the skater. It would have done no good, because no two individuals ever see the same gremlin anyway.

But Fifi was my favorite, and she spent hours sitting right in the center of the artificial horizon, always after dark and usually when the guy in the other seat was napping. She was perfectly proportioned, though barely two inches in height. She always wore shorts or what later came to be known as a miniskirt. She was the epitome of decorum and kept her legs crossed and cased in white knee-length boots, as she idly swung a foot forward and back. She always wore a cap, reminiscent of Robin Hood, with a long feather. Both the cap and the feather regularly changed contrasting colors — the cap scarlet, the feather white; the cap blue, the feather gold; the cap green, the feather violet. I liked this last combination best, because violet was the exact color of her eyes. To hear the tinkling laugh I only had to wink at her. We spent countless hours over the Pacific, and when I no longer had to fly those routes, she was the only thing from that time that I ever missed.

It occurs to me that the "boneyard" at Davis-Monthan Air Base near Tucson, where surplus aircraft are stored, must have literally hundreds of gremlin residents in all those planes scattered for miles in every direction. While planes may pass on, there is no evidence that gremlins ever do. I imagine that their get-togethers would certainly rival the conventions of the River Rats — those fighter pilots who flew over Hansi and the Yalu River.

Incidents: Air
Clark Field, Luzon, Philippine Islands
August 1945

There was a time on approach to Clark Field when a navigator, just arrived from the States, found the Very pistol. This device was designed to be fired only after being inserted into a port in the ceiling of the cockpit, thus insuring that the explosive charge would occur outside the aircraft. This flight officer experienced one trial-and-error learning regarding the proper place to discharge a flare. Moments after he pulled the trigger, a red burst exploded against the back of the copilot's seat.

My problem began immediately when the cockpit filled with a blinding smoke. I grabbed the oxygen mask and tried to keep the plane on course and at the appropriate rate of descent, though the instrument panel was quickly obscured. I could see the flare burning even in the thick smoke, and I knew that it would melt right through the cabin floor. I had a vision of melting control cables resulting in loss of flight control. There was but one thought: get it on the ground before that happened. We opened the side windows to disperse the smoke, producing a display that impressed the tower, for two red flares came arching skyward.

"C-46 on approach, plane on fire. Do you declare emergency?"

I would like to have answered, but I was too busy trying to stay lined up with the runway by the occasional glimpses that I could get out of the left side window, while the copilot was attempting a similar performance on the right side. We brought the aircraft in, made a smooth landing, and were immediately surrounded by crash vehicles.

The landing, I later realized, was by "transferred learning" from cadet flying, where one never got a forward view of the runway while in the rear seat at touchdown. The flare had burned completely through both the cockpit floor and the outer skin of the fuselage. There was paperwork to fill out, and I heard that the navigator was charged for the flare. We never knew, for no one on the crew ever saw that flight officer again.

There was also a time, on another approach to landing at Clark, when I was in the lead plane of a group of 18 C-46s returning for what we hoped would be a rest after repeated resupply runs to Okinawa. We had been flying around the clock for four days on shuttle runs, while trying to nap en route or when our planes were being loaded and unloaded at both ends of the run. Going in, we carried items to make war — bombs, guns, jeeps; coming back, we too often carried the residuals of combat — wounded men and broken equipment.

The last leg of this flight had been on instruments all the way, which meant no naps for either of us. As I entered the pattern and turned on base, my only thought was that in an hour I could sleep. We hadn't been able to get radio clearance to land because the tower frequency was monopolized by a newly arrived Mexican fighter squadron that chattered constantly, overriding all other transmissions. The scuttlebutt was that the next day they took the radios out of the Mexican planes. Whatever, we never heard all that prattling again.

As I turned on approach, a red Aldus signal followed by a red flare got our immediate attention. At that moment, the tower transmission broke through the Mexican babble with, "Army 46 on north landing approach, be advised an AT-6 approaching for a landing from the north."

On the chance I would be heard, I came back with something like the following: "Clark tower, this is the Army 46 on approach to the north. I'm leading a whole group of 46s flown by tired pilots. We are not going to change our landing direction because of that little training plane. Advise the AT-6 to get with it or he and I will be playing chicken on your runway. I want to meet the idiot who's flying that -6 when we land."

My message got through the transmission clutter because the AT-6 turned away, and we had a clear runway. As I was buttoning up, filling out the forms, etc., a corporal drove up with the message, "Lieutenant, you're wanted in Operations. I'll give you a lift."

The Operations officer, a major, greeted me with a solemn look and the statement, "I followed your landing approach and agree with what you did, considering the planes involved and that the AT-6 was trying to land downwind. The problem is that the -6 is being flown by two generals, a two-star and a one-star, getting their four hours for flight pay this month. They asked to meet with you here when they land."

And so I waited with some apprehension, since I had never been geographically close, let alone on speaking terms, with even a one-star, much less a two-star, general. All too soon, everyone in Operations responded to "Attention" as they entered. Their "At ease, men" didn't make me feel comfortable.

I guess you get to be a general by being able to read the signs, because without prompting, although I was probably the most unhappy-looking pilot in the place, the major general put out his hand and said, "Lieutenant, I want you to meet the idiot that was flying that AT-6. In that instance, your judgment was a lot better than mine and you are to be congratulated."

All I could say was, "Thank you, Sir." Then I slept 14 hours.

Nervous in the Service

We had finally moved the squadron to Clark Field as it was then considered "Secure," a euphemism used by higher Headquarters, which was always located at least two islands behind the front. For us "Secure" had come to mean that it was unlikely that there would be a fire fight on the runway while we were landing. This in no way guaranteed that runways still in the process of construction would be clear of bulldozers, however. Coincidentally with landing on a newly secured field, we were supposed to follow a HQ's concept of "the order of exiting the plane." This idea was based on the notion that snipers operated on the assumption that once the plane was parked, navigators usually got off first and pilots last. Because we were told that officers were supposed to be more valuable than enlisted men, we were directed to alter the order of debarkation. Needless to say, this was one of the directives from above to which we paid no attention, other than to complain about the stupidity of back-area paper shufflers.

Bitching about everything, because everything could be legitimately bitched about, had become an art, and one lieutenant I'll call "Joe," after spending two years in the Southwest Pacific, had become a virtuoso. He complained about the food, the climate, the Army in all its manifestations, the living quarters, having to go to bed, having to get up. Clark Field offered him exceptional opportunities to gripe, for we had to set up tents in a muddy area surrounded by cogan grass. While it was always humid, and because this had once been a rice paddy, there was no potable water, except that from chlorine-dosed Lister bags, 50-gallon canvas pouches holding water treated with chlorine tablets, which often reached a temperature of 120 degrees. At night the mosquitos spread malaria with abandon, despite mosquito nets over the folding cots on which we tried to sleep.

I was the only pilot in my squadron who did not contract malaria, though I had the opportunity to observe its effect many times. If lucky, the individual would get the shakes, be too hot, too cold, dehydrate, and experience massive discomfort requiring medical attention — and after a time appear to recover completely. If unlucky, malaria struck at the brain, producing bizarre symptoms. On two occasions, once in the Philippines and once in Japan, I got involved in trying to get a compatriot to surrender his .45 and forestall the intention "to shoot anything that moved." In the incident in Japan, I got the gun on my promise to let the lieutenant jump out of a second-story window. Once I got the gun, I "cold-cocked" him, and we shipped him off to the hospital. Both of these individuals went Stateside for intensive treatment.

With the bugs and the heat, sleep would have been difficult enough, but there was more. It seems that the Japanese had not received the message from our Headquarters informing them that they were no longer a threat to us, so they kept doing their thing. Their "thing" consisted of waiting till after midnight, when they would creep through the high grass, coming close enough to roll grenades into our tents. This behavior definitely interrupted pleasant dreams and interfered with tranquil slumber. We kept our .45s under the pillow and a submachine-gun under the cot. At the sound of the first explosion, we were up and out to an assigned position on the surrounding dike, where in unison, on signal, we often emptied magazines of Thompson .45s into the high grass. The next morning the MPs would search the area for Japanese bodies, and they usually found some. Suffice it to say, we got a lot more of them than they got of us, which is one way that those in Headquarters keep score. We concluded early on that those who declare areas secure are not the same individuals who keep track of enemy casualties.

After one especially active night, I joined Joe in the mess tent for morning coffee. As usual, I expected to hear him bitch about the absence of infantry support so that we could get some sleep, for just the week before he had told me that he had enlisted in the Air Corps to avoid being an infantry dogface. Joe didn't say a word. He didn't drink his coffee. He just sat there with what came to be known as "the thousand-yard stare," as depicted in artist Tom Lea's well-known portrait of a Marine suffering from combat fatigue. I already knew that when the bitching stops it means trouble, so I suggested that he go see the flight surgeon. He just looked blankly at me.

I went to see the doctor with my tale of the sudden change in Joe's demeanor. Though a major, this man had a manner more typical of a family doctor than that of a superior officer, which meant that he was ideally suited for an Air Corps outfit. He examined Joe and made a diagnosis of "lack-anookie" with the prescription that Joe seek the services of one of the Filipino ladies, who had built their grass huts next to our squadron area. The doctor's prescription for Joe was no secret to the rest of the squadron, and we were all anxious for his recovery. We just wanted to hear him talk again. There was some speculation that Joe might still be a virgin, but, so what, as he was being ordered to take the cure.

Trying not to be conspicuous, everyone watched as Joe approached a nearby hut. As was the custom, the hut was covered with palm branches and raised on stilts to prevent intruding vermin. Though he appeared sheepish, Joe resolutely climbed the steps and went inside. Now it was quite apparent that everyone in the outfit had viewed his entrance to the hut and was eagerly waiting to assess the effects of the prescribed remedy. But after a period of time, some of the group grew tired of waiting for the results. They approached and peeked, for there was no door. Pleased with their finding, they decided that everyone should see, so they lifted the hut onto their shoulders and carried it to the center of the compound. Then they removed the sides to reveal the occupants busily engaged.

There was cheering. Joe not only noticed, he stood naked on the platform and cursed everyone and everything, alive and dead. All branches of the service were included, with special emphasis on the Air Corps and Troop Carrier. His bitching had acquired a new grandeur. The treatment had worked. Joe was cured.

Incidents: Ground
Clark Field, Luzon, Philippine Islands

Even when not in the air, pilots are curious about any plane, any time, any place. So it was that the following exchanges occurred.

An entirely new wing of Douglas A-26 Invaders twin-engine planes arrived from the States, and once lined up on the ramp, they began to draw a crowd. All bright shining silver, the Invader was sleek, conceived for a lethal purpose, and designed to attack. At speeds in excess of 370 mph, this plane could bring to bear six .50-calibers in the nose plus ten more in side blisters and on under-wing pylons while carrying 4,000 pounds of bombs. As an alternate, the under-wing pylons could accommodate 16 rockets. At that time and place, this new addition looked better than sliced bread, and so it was that I parked my jeep in front of the lead plane and got out to investigate.

A figure in fatigues with his head down was busily engaged in adjusting something in the cockpit. I hollered, "Hey, when are you going to get those things in the war?"

A muffled voice responded, "I'll be with you in a minute, as soon as I get this fixed."

In moments he was face to face with me and obviously eager to answer my questions. But I was tongue-tied, because this new acquaintance, no matter that I learned later he was 28 and only 8 years my senior, had the silver star of a brigadier general on his fatigue cap. For a 2nd lieutenant to associate with generals is one hell of a jump, or so I thought, until I came to know this gentleman. Not only was he gracious, but he was also anxious to show off his aircraft. The fact that we were both pilots took precedence over every other convention, for those who fly do belong to a special fraternity.

That a 28-year-old could achieve the status of general was not only testimony to his ability, but also reflected both the high combat casualty rate and the quantitative expansion of the Army Air Corps. I believe that George

B-24 *The Dragon and His Tail*, at Clark Field, PI.

Custer was about the same age when he made brevet general in the Civil War and under similar circumstances. I don't know how this Air Corps general fared, but the A-26 went on to fight in Korea and Vietnam.

Another time, parked on the ramp at Clark Field was a big, black aircraft. Painted on the fuselage, under the cockpit window, were two Japanese flags, indicating enemy planes destroyed; two ships in silhouette, sinking; and one bicycle.

The plane was a PB4Y-2 Navy Privateer, a long-range bomber and/or reconnaissance version with nose guns, as well as two dorsal, a tail turret, and two waist blister guns — all .50 caliber. In addition, the plane carried 8,000 pounds of bombs.

What about the bike? Of course, that's the first question I asked. The answer, to summarize what several of the crew tried to explain simultaneously:

> We were over one of the southern Japanese islands and there was a guy on a bicycle, peddling as fast as he could. The tail gunner asked for a chance to test his marksmanship, and we made a pass. He missed, and the bike kept going. Before we were done, everyone had an individual chance, for we made a half dozen passes. We had never worked this hard to sink a ship, and everyone was embarrassed at the lack of accuracy. On our final pass, we caught the bicycle crossing a bridge, which we destroyed with a 500-pound bomb. As a claim, the bicycle seemed more appropriate than a bridge.

Also on the ramp was one of the most famous airplanes in the Southwest Pacific theater. It was a B-24 Liberator, a standard model. What made it unique was the artistic rendition that depicted its name, *The Dragon and His Tail.* Although many planes had nose art, this artistic creation began just aft of the nose turret and extended some 70 feet back to the rudders. A red-headed, nude female with ample breasts was held in the claws of a leering green dragon, whose body was large enough to cover over half of the main fuselage, while the tip of his tail curled on the rudder.

In the air, this particular plane was often a menace, because pilots, especially if they were from a different field, wanted a close look. They would fly formation without invitation. And if several were involved, traffic problems quickly developed, as each vied for his turn at art appreciation. At the time, this magnetic attraction stemmed from the fact that there was a distinct shortage of things to laugh about.

B-24 *Mad Russian.*

B-24 *Cocktail Hour*, Clark Field, PI.

Nose art of B-24 *Million $ Baby,* Clark Field, PI.

On this same ramp there was a B-24 whose fuselage was adorned by a lithe, shapely, scantily clad female with high heels and a top hat, cocked at a saucy angle, which complimented her seductive facial expression. Her shapely legs only partially obscured a Manhattan cocktail, which was nearly her equal in size. In the background there were stars and musical notes, while the cherry in the Manhattan was taking flight, as tiny wings propelled it upward. The ship carried the name *Cocktail Hour*.

Neighboring B-24s also sported individual art with names such as *Mad*

B-24 *The Red-headed Rebel,* Clark Field, PI.

Russian, The Read-headed Rebel, Million $ Baby; in each instance, the females depicted had spectacular figures. Conclusions? First, airplanes are always considered feminine in gender; second, air crews have a special affinity for attractive females.

During this time, U.S. air crews dropped propaganda leaflets throughout the Philippine Islands that were actually summaries of news headline stories from across the world. We called them the "Parachute News."

May 5, 1945

#1. Rome, May 3 — Mussolini executed — Mussolini and his lover were executed. His body, along with those of fifteen other fascists, was exposed in public in Milano. His death brought about the end of fascism in Italy, thus ensuring the reconstruction of that country.

#2. Manila, May 4 — Military facilities bombed — Last week, military facilities in Taiwan were bombed continuously by U.S. bombers out of the Philippines. Airports, forts, and the naval base on the northern shore were bombed and destroyed. A 1,000-ton cargo ship was bombed and sunk near northern Luzon. Many other cargo ships were sunk [*in other areas*].

#3. Manila, May 4 — Twenty-one ships sunk. Continent bombed repeatedly — Last week, U.S. bombers out of the Philippines sunk 21 mainly small cargo ships in the China Sea and bombed several areas on the Asian continent repeatedly. U.S. Air Forces planes attacked military bases in Saigon twice, dropping 250 one-ton high-explosive bombs, destroying buildings, including an alcohol factory.

Island outposts in the Malay offing were bombed.

#4. Manila, May 4 — Japanese princess Masako married one week ago.

#5. Paris, May 3 — History is made when the U.S. and Soviet Union decide to cooperate.

Germany divided.

Soviet occupies three quarters of Berlin.

#6. Rome, May 3 — German line in Northern Italy is broken — Allied forces broke the German line in northern Italy. Naval bases in Italy were taken.

#7. Manila, May 4 — Japanese Imperial rescript to the Japanese people — [*Due to copy quality this article cannot be read.*]

Propaganda leaflet

昭和二十年五月五日(土曜日) 落下傘ニュース 第八號 (第一頁)

落下傘ニュース

米軍マニラ司令部發行

1

ム氏處刑さる

【ローマ三日發】イタリーの獨裁者たりしベニト・ムッソリーニ氏は先週イタリー志士軍に逮捕せられミラノ市の近郊に於て民衆裁判の結果遂に處刑せられた、ムッソリーニ氏の愛人も亦同様處刑せられ遺骸は他のファシスト黨員十五名の遺骸と共に聯合軍の入城に先立ちミラノ市に於て公衆の面前に曝された、ムッソリーニ氏は二年前聯合軍がイタリーに上陸作戰中に失脚、彼の廿一年間に及ぶ獨裁權を失つた、其後ドイツに逃避し昨年ドイツの保護下に北イタリーに歸つて來たのであつた、ムッソリーニ氏を死刑に處した北伊委員會は、獨裁者の死は廿年間に亘る武力による權力の横奪を終焉せしめ、イタリーの再生と再建とを約束したものであると述べてゐる

4

正子殿下御結婚

【マニラ四日發】同盟通信の報道によれば、今上陛下の皇女正子内親王殿下には先週、龍田德彦侯と御婚禮を擧げさせられた

5

米ソ兩軍の歷史的連結成る
獨逸本土を寸斷
ソ軍伯林の四分の三を占據

【パリ三日發】東西よりドイツ國内を横斷進擊した聯合軍は先週遂にベルリンの南百二十粁の地點に於て連結した、その間聯合軍は至る處で、曾てその威を誇つた獨軍殘存部隊を寸斷した、この連結はソ軍と米第一軍との間になされたのであつた

一方ベルリン市内のソ軍電擊部隊は同市を十重二十重に取り圍んで市の四分の三を手中に收め、ナチ防衛軍を市の中央部に追ひ込んだ

また南ドイツの米軍は、オーストリヤ國内に進擊し、イタリーの關門であるブレンネル峠まで六十粁の地點に到達した

他の米軍部隊はナチ誕生の地ミユンヘンに迫り戰車部隊はチエコスロバキヤに進擊した

なほ又、北部ドイツの英軍はブレーメン市を占領した、同市はドイツ第二の港であり又潜水艦基地である、その後英軍は包圍下にあるハンブルグ市の傍を通過、バルチック海に向つて進擊した、北海沿岸のカナダ軍は要港エムデンを距る六粁の地點に迫り、同港の姉妹港ウイルヘルムスハーヘンに脅威を與へるに至つた

ドイツ
ブレメン
ベルリン
露軍
英軍
米軍
佛軍
チエッコスロバキヤ
露軍
ブレンネル峠
オーストリヤ

6

北伊戰線の獨軍崩壞

【ローマ三日發】北伊戰線に於けるドイツ軍は先週、聯合軍の反復猛攻擊により崩壞した、聯合軍は要港ゼノア並にスペチア海軍基地を占領し、更に義勇軍により既に占領されてゐたベニス並にミラノに入城した

7

國民に御詔勅

(マニラ四日發) マニラで聽取せる同盟放送によれば、先週天皇陛下には、空襲下の罹災民に對して御内帑金を御下賜遊ばされたがその際國民に賜はれる勅語の一部は次の如し

『戰局愈々危急ニ赴キ、敵ノ我カ國土ヲ侵襲スル漸ク苛烈ヲ加フ。朕カ赤子ニシテ、或ハ非命ニ斃レ、傷痍ニ苦ミ、或ハ家財ヲ失ヒ職業ニ離レ、其ノ生ヲ聊ンセサル者アルヲ見ルハ、朕ノ軫念措ク能ハサルトコロナリ茲ニ内帑ノ金ヲ出シ之カ救恤、振作ノ資ニ充テシム……』

8

獨軍の捕虜二百四十万

【パリ三日發】先週の聯合軍最高司令部發表によれば、西部戰線に於て捕虜となつた獨軍は、二百四十万以上に達した、そのうち百万人以上のナチ軍はこの四月精强な聯合軍が獨本國を席捲した際捕虜となつたものである

2

台灣の各軍事施設を猛連爆

【マニラ四日發】比島基地よりの米爆撃機隊は先週台灣を連日强襲、各地飛行場、砲台及び北岸にある淡水海軍基地を爆破した、同隊は又ルソン島の北方バタン諸島で一千屯級貨物船を撃沈、また南西諸島沖で貨物船五隻を撃沈し、澎湖島の近くで四隻を撃沈した

台灣空襲の目標は同島西南の恒春、屏東、高雄各地區における飛行場及び軍事施設と松山、台南、カムカ、花蓮港等の飛行場であつた、又台東、恒春、屏東の軍需工場及び台南、北港の鐵道操車場も爆撃された

米機の攻擊に油槽船爆發—澎湖島馬公日本海軍基地にて

9

B29空前の猛爆
四國をも初爆擊

【グアム四日發】超「空の要塞」の大群は先週末引續き四日間に亘り、マリアナ基地から、日本本土に對して、未曾有の連續大爆擊を敢行した本爆擊の主な目的は日本航空力の擊碎にあり、先づ沖縄の米軍飛行基地を常に脅かしつつある九州の各飛行場に對して爆擊を加へた、この空中大艦隊の攻擊には、B29が連日二百五十機も參加したこの爆擊で、國分が四回宮崎及び都城が三回和泉及び串良が各二回に亘り攻擊され、更に又四國の西北岸松山市に對してもB29による最初の爆擊が行はれた、その他、鹿屋、宇佐(大分)、佐伯、富高新田ケ原及び東鹿屋に對しても爆擊を加へた

尚先週初めB29の一隊は東京の西廿二粁の立川にある日立飛行機工場をも爆擊した、この攻擊に於て日本の戰鬪機卅一機を擊墜したが米軍も亦B29四機を失つた

3

船舶廿一隻を擊沈
大陸をも反覆爆擊

【マニラ四日發】比島基地の爆擊機隊は先週支那沿岸沖で、主として小型貨物船廿一隻を擊沈、アジア大陸各地を連續爆擊した

米航空機はサイゴンの海軍基地を二回に亘り爆擊、二百五十一噸の高性爆彈を投下し船渠、建物等を破壞、アルコール製造工場を大破させた、同隊は又船渠に於て貨物船一隻を擊破、三千噸の貨物船に火災を起させ又潜水艦一隻に至近彈を浴せた、尚海南島の楡林港攻擊に際しては四千噸級貨物船一隻、小型貨物船三隻及び鉄舟十五隻を擊沈した他の爆擊機隊は西貢の北方及び印度支那沿岸に沿ふ鉄道を爆擊損害を與へた、最後にマレー沖にある前哨地點の施設をも爆擊した

米空軍基地芷江を脅威

【重慶四日發】支那軍當局の戰況公報によれば先週、五ケ師團の日本軍は西部湖南省の米軍航空基地、芷江を距る約百粁の地點に進出した

10

バギオ占領
カ谿谷に今一歩

【マニラ四日發】米軍は先週遂に、バギオ市を占領した、同市は比島の夏の都として知られ、北部ルソン山嶽地帶にあつて海拔千六百米、昨日までマニラ撤收後の山下大將の最高司令部所在地であつた、マッカーサー將軍は同市の陷落は歩兵、砲兵、戰車、飛行機の綜合攻擊の結果であると語つた

又ルソン地區の他の米軍は嶮しい山岳地帶で夜襲を試み乍ら遂にカガヤン谿谷入口であるバレテ峠を一目で見下す要衝を占據した、他方米空軍は同谿谷の日本軍陣地に千二百五十噸の爆彈をたたき込んだ、比島軍も亦空軍の協力下に西海岸のビガンを占領した、なほマッカーサー將軍は南イロコス地方が、一部の孤立した日本軍敗殘兵に對する掃蕩戰を除いて全く米軍の手に歸した旨發表した

ラングーンまで五十粁

【カルカッタ四日發】先週僅か廿四時間以内に一躍九〇粁を南下突進した英軍戰車隊は、ビルマの首都であり最大の要港であるラングーンまであと五十粁の地點に進出した

14

ダバオに廿七粁
比人部隊も活躍

【マニラ四日發】ミンダナオ島に於ける、マッカーサー將軍麾下の諸部隊は、先週同島最大の都市ダバオ要港まで廿七粁の地點に進入した

即ち二週間前にミンダナオ西海岸に上陸した米軍部隊は、戰鬪を續けながらダバオ灣デイゴス附近へ進軍、更に南北へ進出した、北進の部隊は、高射砲の精巧なる防禦陣や沿岸防備陣等を蹂躪した又南進部隊はバタダ飛行場を占據、米軍機は既に之を使用してゐる、なほ比島軍部隊は、ダバオ近傍のタリクド島を占領しまた海軍の輕艦艇はダバオ市附近の海岸防備施設を砲擊した

中部ミンダナオに於ける米軍部隊は、幹線道路を北進し、カバカンの北に出た

13

新生日本の爲に

【マニラ四日發】目下比島某所に收容中の一日本高級將校は先週落下傘ニュースの記者に次の樣に語つた、「一九四二年バターンで米軍の捕虜となつた日本の將兵達は、その後日本軍が同地を占據した爲救出せられたが、彼等は日本軍から何等の恥辱も壓迫をも受けなかつた」某將校は更に語る「此の際米軍は、比島に孤立せる日本軍に對して、もつと宣傳文を投下し、將校をしてかれらの部下を抗戰による無益な死に陥れるよりは、むしろ戰鬪を中止させる方がかれらの眞にとるべき責任であると訴へるべきである、この事は戰後日本の再建の爲に、國民の華、青年を生き殘らせる事であり、日本の將來の爲に最も必要な事なのである」

12

桑港會議開幕
新世界を設計

【サンフランシスコ四日發】戰後の世界平和機構を確立するための聯合國會議は、四十六ケ國の代表者を迎へて先週サンフランシスコで開かれた、米大統領ツルーマン氏は各國代表者に歡迎の辭を述べて彼等こそ「より良き世界の設計者」であると讃へ、各國民の嘗つた戰爭の大なる犧牲を償ふに足る立派な平和を出現させるべきであると要請、最後に「我々は此の機會に再び戰爭が起らない樣對策を決定せねばならない」と結んだ

11

米軍、那覇市防衛第一線を突破

【グアム四日發】沖縄南部戰線の米軍は先週那覇市の日本軍第一防禦陣を突破し第二壘陣地を强襲した、一方西海岸に於ては米軍はマチナト飛行場の傍まで進出又同戰線の他の部隊はヨナバル飛行場の北高地を占據した

米軍は更に前進を續け然に首都那覇へ五粁、そして沖縄第二の都市、首里へ三粁の地點に到達した

ニミッツ提督の發表によれば、四月一日米軍沖縄上陸以來日本軍の損害は戰死二万一千二百六十九名に達した

（第二頁）　第八號　落下傘ニュース　昭和二十年五月五日（土曜日）

⑮

硫黄島收容所訪問記
千名の捕虜
溫い保護に更生の毎日

米軍から食事を貰ふ日本人母子 ——沖繩島で

【ニューヨーク三日發】硫黄島に從軍してゐるヘラルド・トリビューン紙記者の報道によれば、同島で約一千名の日本軍將兵が捕虜となつたといふこのうち約半數は先月自發的に米軍の保護下に入つたもので、海軍病院部隊全員もこの中に含まれてゐる、米軍の手中にある日本軍將兵は米軍の食料と毎日一個の煙草を給與され、その他醫療手當と清潔な睡眠場所とを與へられてゐる

トリビューン紙記者は捕虜收容所訪問記を次の如く書いてゐる

「吾々を案内してくれたフランシス・マーフィ軍曹はこの收容所に日本人が約千名ゐると教へてくれた、この收容所は逃げようと思へば樂に逃げられるにもかかはらず、いまだに一人として許可なしに外に出ようとしたものはない

マーフィ軍曹はまたから言つてゐた、〃最初捕へられて此所に連れられて來た當座は、殺されるのではないかとか或はひどい目に遭はされるのではないかとかこのやうに誰もが間違ひなく考へてゐた[illegible]に捕虜となつてゐる人々から話を聞いて急に元氣になるのだ、それから、かれらの半分は再び山に戻つて、いまだに潜伏してゐるかれらの仲間を連れ歸つて來たいといふ志願者である〃

吾々は將校だけが入つてゐるキャンプで若い大尉に會つた、かれは多數の兵隊に說いて米軍の保護を受けさせるに成功したといふ

捕虜達は自分達で炊事をし收容所の庭の手入れをしてゐる、かれらの世話を燒いてゐるのは五十一才の老中尉である、かれは兵隊上りで戰爭が始まるまでは一軍曹に過ぎなかつた、いまかれは日本軍の制服を着、茶脚絆を着け軍帽を被つて、用事のときには收容所を出たり入つたりすることを許されてゐる」

⑯

淺草、日本橋など
十七區壞滅
その他の地區も被害甚大

【マニラ四日發】マニラで聽取せる同盟放送によれば、三月以來、東京空襲による被害地區は次の如し、「淺草、本所、深川、向島の各區は全滅し、下谷、本鄉、日本橋、神田、荒川の各區は甚大な損害を被つた、尙、豐島、板橋、王子、四谷、大森、荏原、品川の各區も四月に行はれた空襲により相當な被害を受けた、蒲田區はその大半も大損害を蒙り、その他の地域にも若干の損害があつた」

⑰

年に百万噸餘投下

【サイパン四日發】先週U・P・特派員の報道によれば、昨年英基地の米軍機がドイツを爆擊したと同量の爆彈を、B29だけで今年中に日本に對しばら撒くであらうといはれてゐる

聯合軍がヨーロッパ大陸に侵入し、ドイツ軍を擊破した昨一九四四年には米軍機だけで、ドイツの頭上に百十万噸の爆彈を投下してゐる

マリアナ群島に於けるB29の指揮官は、日本本土に六十万噸の爆彈投下を計劃する樣命ぜられてゐる旨語つてゐるが、支那に基地を有するB29機群も、同量の爆彈を投下するものと見られてゐる

最近のB29四百機による空襲は、毎回三千噸宛の爆彈を投下してゐる

マニラ放送

毎日午後五時半（日本時間）からニュースを送ります　九二九五粁サイクル、三二・二七米にお合せ下さい

㉔

縣知事以下百卅五名の大量人事

【マニラ四日發】先週の同盟通信によれば、今回内務省管下百三十五名の縣知事及び幹部級の異動が行はれた、これは開戰以來最大の人事異動であるが、この異動で元警視總監丸山鶴吉氏は宮城縣知事に任命された、丸山氏は曾て同縣知事を勤めたことがあり從つて、今回は再任である、このほか三重縣知事持永義夫氏は兵庫縣知事に、滋賀縣知事菊池守人氏は靜岡縣知事に任命された

⑱

日本海軍を敗る米移動海軍基地

【ワシントン四日發】先週米海軍省は移動海軍基地の活躍に關し次の如く述べた、比島、硫黄島、沖繩作戰で米軍が成功したのは太平洋を數千粁に亘つて活躍する兵站船、修理船の〃橋〃があつたからである、これらの船舶は移動海軍基地となつた即ち艦隊と共に行動し、而もその艦隊をして世界のどの海軍よりも長期間海上に止まることを可能にしたのである、レイテ灣で昨年十月、日本の海軍が敗れたのはかういふ兵站船が米艦隊に從いてゐたからである、日本の海軍は米艦隊がやがて[illegible]數週間の後には彈藥燃料に不足するものと信じて攻擊して來た、ところが米艦隊は豐富な補給を受けてゐてレイテ灣の大海戰には日本艦隊が逆に擊沈破されたのである

⑲

スキー場を畑に

【マニラ四日發】群馬縣の有名な藤間スキー場も近く畑として更生し約十町歩に芋、玉蜀黍が作られて食料增產に一役買ふことになつた＝先週の同盟ニュース

㉑

バギオ作戰側面奇襲成功
第卅三師

【マニラ四日發】先週の前線報道によれば米第卅三師團は側面奇襲作戰を敢行の後アシン、バギオ街道に沿ふてバギオ市境界線内に突進した

即ち、山下大將麾下の指揮官は右街道上の二つのトンネルと附近高地の要衝を防衛、之によつて米軍の强襲を防がんとしたこのため正面からする米軍の攻擊は數回に亘り日本軍に擊退されたこの攻擊で日本軍が疲勞困憊してゐる間に米軍の他の部隊はトンネルの北の一地點に向つてナギリヤン道路を進擊、日本軍を包圍するの態勢に出たため日本軍はバギオに向つて退却を余儀なくされた

尙日本軍は水道管を破壞したため街道の一部は流失したが米軍工兵隊は直ちに修理作業を成し遂げ攻擊部隊のバギオ進擊を可能にした

㉒

市内に突入
第卅七師

【マニラ四日發】米軍前線記者の報道によれば先週米軍は、避暑地バギオに對して最後の攻擊を加へ日本軍と猛烈なる山獄戰を演じた

即ち米卅七師團の精銳は夜間、戰車二台を有する日本軍の烈しい逆襲を受けたが之れを擊退、市の中央部に突入したのであつた

㉓

らが本當？

【マニラ廿日發】最近マニラで聽取した東京放送は次のやうな全く正反對の聲明をしてゐる、即ち三月十三日の放送に曰く「東京が完全に焦土となれば火事に對する懸念は全く無くなり我々はもつとよく戰ふことが出來るであらう」

三月廿日の放送に曰く「我々は各都市を敵の爆擊下に曝してこれを焦土となすわけには行かぬ、日本の生產工業はこれ等の都會に集中してゐる、これを防禦することは戰爭遂行上絕對に必要である」

㉕

歐洲進擊史
米ソ兩軍合流
攻擊卅ケ月の成果

【ロンドン三日發】先週ベルリン近郊に於いてソ聯軍と西部戰線の聯合軍とは遂に連結、斯て世界戰史に類例のない强力なる二大軍隊が一地點に會するに至つたこれこそまさに約八百万人の軍隊を擁する聯合軍の卅ケ月に亘る攻擊の最高潮の場であつた、この精强な聯合軍は、一時九百万人の大軍を有した侵略的ナチ帝國を擊碎したのである、即ち

この二年半の間、聯合軍は、曾て東西三千二百粁（大西洋からボルガ河まで）、南北六千五百粁（ノルウエーから西アフリカのダカールまで）、に亘つて暴れ廻つたドイツ陸軍を粉碎したのであつた、この最初の大攻擊は一九四二年十一月、聯合軍の北アフリカ上陸作戰に始まり續いて六ケ月間にアフリカの樞軸軍は一人殘らず驅逐せられ、而もこの間ソ軍はスターリングラードでドイツ軍を打破したのであつた、因みにこのスターリングラードの一戰こそ今次大戰の天王山であつたのである、一九四三年九月にはイタリーの敗戰となり、イタリー艦隊は降服した、然して英國に基地を有つ大聯合軍のフランス上陸が開始されて間もなく一九四四年六月イタリーの首府ローマは陷落したのである

本年の初めまでにフランスとベルギーのほとんど大半が平定され、曾つて精强を誇つた獨軍の殘存部隊もヂークフリード要塞線にまで押戻され一方ソ聯軍はフィンランド、ルーマニヤ、ブルガリヤ及ハンガリーを降伏させた、又一度はロシヤ國內深く二千五百粁も侵入したヒットラー軍はベルリンの城門にまで追ひつめられた

先月ライン河を渡河した聯合軍はソ軍と合流する[illegible]んだ、そして、先週遂に合流した大軍は爆擊で破壞されたドイツの首府ベルリン市――これこそは曾つてナチスにより世界制覇が企てられたその本據なのだ――の內外に殺到したのである

⑳

超「空の要塞」日本の軍事施設を爆擊

#8. Paris, May 3 — Number of German POWs reaches 2.4 million.

#9. Guam, May 4 — B-29s pound Japan in unprecedented fashion — Shikoku was bombed for the first time. Superfortresses out of Manila bombed the Japanese mainland continuously for four days. The object of the attack was the destruction of Japan's air force. Airports in Kyushu, which threatened U.S. air bases in Okinawa, were bombed. 250 B-29s participated in the bombing. Early last week, B-29s bombed the Hitachi airplane factory in Tachikawa, Tokyo. During this attack, one Japanese fighter was shot down, while four B-29s were lost.

#10. Manila, May 4 — Baguio occupied — Last week the U.S. Army occupied Baguio, a city known as the "summer capital." Until yesterday, it was General Yamashita's supreme headquarters.

#11. Guam, May 4 — U.S. Army breaks through Japan's defensive line in Naha City, Okinawa — U.S. Army reaches Naha and Shuri. According to a commander, 21,269 Japanese people have been killed since the U.S. Army landed in Okinawa on April 1. [*The commander mentioned is General Mitsuri Ushijima.*]

#12. San Francisco, May 4 — Conference held in San Francisco — Last week in San Francisco 46 nations met to discuss world peace. Truman indicated his desire for the development of policies which would prevent war in the future.

#13. Manila, May 4 — For the New Japan — A captured Japanese officer in the Philippines told this reporter that the U.S. should continue dropping the "Parachute News" throughout the Philippines. The surrender of the Japanese soldiers still in the Philippines will prevent the loss of many lives, and will aid the reconstruction of Japan in the future.

#14. Manila, May 4 — U.S. reaches Dabao — [*Probably refers to Davao, Mindanao, PI.*]

#15. New York, May 3 [*1945*] — A visit to Iwo Jima prison camp — One thousand war captives — According to a war reporter with the *Herald Tribune,* who is on Iwo Jima, about 1,000 soldiers have been captured. About half that number surrendered on their own volition. Those in the naval hospital are also included in this number. Food and cigarettes are given to the Japanese captives every day. Medical care and clean quarters are provided. This war correspondent wrote about his visit to this camp. Sergeant Francis Murphy told him that there are 1,000 Japanese in this camp. These men could escape easily if they desired, but no one has attempted to do so. At first, the Japanese captives feared ill treatment, but once they heard about the situation in the camp from those who had already spent time there, they were relieved. Some of them returned to the mountains where their fellows were hiding and brought them back to camp. We met a young captain who was successful in persuading his men to enter the protection of the U.S.

Captives usually cook for themselves, and take care of a garden in the camp.

#16. Manila, May 4 — Seventeen wards including Asakusa and Nihonbashi destroyed — Other wards also badly damaged — According to an Allied radio broadcast, the areas damaged by the Tokyo air raid are as follows: (destroyed completely) Asakusa, Honjo, Fukagawa, Mukojima, (badly damaged) Hongo, Nihonbashi, Kanda, Arakawa, (damaged considerably) Toshima, Itabashi, Oji, Yotsuya, Oomori, Shinagawa. Kamata and most wards were badly damaged. Other areas were also damaged to some extent.

#17. Saipan, May 4 — More than one million tons of bombs will be dropped on Japan this year — According to a UP correspondent last week, the same tonnage dropped on Germany by the U.S. aircraft based in Britain last year will be dropped on Japan this year by B-29s. When the Allied forces invaded Europe in 1944, 1,100,000 tons of bombs were dropped on Germany. The commander of B-29s on the Mariana Islands said that he was ordered to drop 600,000 tons of bombs on Japan. Also aircraft based in China are supposed to drop the same tonnage on Japan. Recent raids by B-29s dropped 3,000 tons of bombs each time.

#18. Washington, May 4 — American mobile naval base defeats Japanese navy — Last week the U.S. Navy talked about the successful American mobile naval base. The reason the U.S. Navy succeeded in the Philippines, Iwo Jima, and Okinawa was the close cooperation between supply ships and repair ships. These ships were very active traveling

> thousands of kilometers across the Pacific Ocean. They operated with the Fleet to stay at sea for record periods of time.
>
> The reason the Japanese navy was defeated at Leyte Gulf last October was because the U.S. had ships like these. The Japanese navy believed that the U.S. Navy would run out of munitions and supplies sooner or later after several weeks of fighting, but the U.S. Fleet had ample supplies from the supply ships. The Japanese navy was defeated despite its expectations.

This particular "paper bomb" was also dropped on Japan. Mr. H. Taniguchi was 12 years old at that time, and in October 1993, he assisted in translating parts of the leaflet, adding the following commentary:

> The Japanese navy had a lot of superb submarines and long-cruising oxygen torpedoes. However, it made fundamental mistakes.
>
> Japanese submarines fought with the Japanese fleet against opponent warships, but they did not attack against transport ships except during the last stage of the war.
>
> The reason Japanese submarines did not attack against opponent transport ships was that the Japanese Samurai (warrior) did not like to attack against an unarmed person.
>
> This is the traditional spirit of Samurai, and it is a sort of mental aesthetics. Their minds did not allow an attack against submarines, called "Long Bridge."
>
> It seems to be a fine attitude at a glance, but I believe it is a sort of vanity.
>
> To supply many goods from its own country to the front lines and keep combat troops in good condition was the basic regular course of the war. If not done, the combat troops would be blasted in a short time. The so-called "War" had such a primary dependence on the importance of transportation.
>
> U.S. submarines sank many Japanese transport ships. I believe it was normal from the strategic point of view. German U-boats sank many U.S. transport ships, too. It was the right way for the same reason.
>
> I think that the Japanese navy did not have a systematic strat-

egy for submarine use. It was an unfortunate matter for Japan's navy.

#19. Manila, May 4 — Skiing course transformed into farm fields — The well known Fujima skiing course of Gumma Prefecture will soon be transformed into fields. Potatoes and corn will be planted helping provide food supplies.

#20. B-29 Superfortress dropping bombs on Japanese military facilities.

#21. Manila, May 4 — Baguio military operation by the 33rd Division in successful flank attack — According to last week's news from the front, the U.S. Army 33rd Division marched along the Asin and Baguio Highway and reached the border of Baguio City after launching attacks upon the flank of the enemy.

A commander under General Yamashita defended the two tunnels on the roads and adjacent heights against the strong U.S. attack. Several U.S. attacks to the Japanese front line failed due to the strong resistance. While the Japanese army was exhausted by continuous U.S. attacks, separate U.S. troops proceeded to the north of the tunnel along the Nagiyan Road to attempt to take the Japanese army on the flank. The Japanese army had no choice but to withdraw to Baguio.

Although the Japanese army destroyed the water supply lines on the way back to Baguio, which flooded some parts of the road, a U.S. Army engineer group immediately restored the road and made possible the U.S. troops advance to Baguio City.

#22. Manila, May 4 — U.S. troops rush into downtown — the 37th Division — A U.S. front-line correspondent reported that last week the U.S. Army made a final attack on Baguio and exchanged fire in mountainous terrain against the Japanese army.

The elite troops of the 37th Division received an intensive night attack from the Japanese army, including two tanks, but drove them back and penetrated into the center of Baguio City.

#23. Manila, May 20 — Which news is true? — Tokyo Radio, monitored in Manila, announced the following contradictory statements:

The broadcast on March 13th said, "If Tokyo is totally burnt and completely demolished, there will be no more fear from fire and the Japanese can concentrate their power into better fighting against the Allies."

The broadcast on March 20th said, "We cannot stand to expose our cities to enemy air raids and let them be demolished. Almost all manufacturing industries are concentrated in these cities. Therefore, it is imperative to protect those cities in order for us to continue the war."

#24. Manila, May 4 — Massive reassignment of 125 prefectural governors and others — According to last week's joint wire service, the Ministry of Internal Affairs undertook the reassignment of 125 prefectural governors and subordinates. These personnel changes were the largest ever since the war broke out.

By this reorganization, Mr. Tsurukichi Maruyama, ex-Superintendent General of Metropolitan Police was assigned to become governor of Miyagi Prefecture. He had been governor of Miyagi once before and thus he returns to his former position. Among others who were affected by these personnel changes were ex-Mie Prefecture Governor, Mr. Yoshio Shimizu, who will become Governor of Hyogo Prefecture, and ex-Shiga Prefecture Governor, Mr. Morito Kikuchi, who will be reassigned to Shizuoka Prefecture.

MANILA RADIO STATION

Every day 5:30 p.m. (Japan Time) the news will be broadcast. Tune to 9,295 KHZ, 32,27m.

#25. London, May 3 — U.S. Army joins with Russian army, Victory after 30 months assault — The Russian army and western front Allied forces were finally united last week on the outskirts of Berlin. This united force consisted of eight million soldiers of the world's two leading armies and was historically the largest ever seen meeting in one place. This scene was the highest point after 30 months of battles.

This same united force at one point had nine million soldiers, which destroyed the invasive Nazi Imperial Empire. During the past two and one-half years, this united force suppressed the German army, which had spread its power 3,200 km east to west (from the Atlantic to the Volga River) and north to south 6,500 km (from Norway to Dakar in West Africa). The first big success was in November 1942, when the united forces landed in North Africa and within six months captured all German soldiers in the region. Around the same time, the Russian army destroyed the German army at Stalingrad. This was the breaking point in the war. In September 1942, the Italians lost the war and the Italian army surrendered. The great Allied force, which was headquartered in England, attacked the Germans in France, and Italy's capital, Rome, fell in June 1944. By the first of the year all of France and Belgium were subdued by the Allied forces and the remaining dispirited German army was pushed back to the Ziegfried Line.

The Russian army freed Finland, Romania, Bulgaria, and Hungary. The Germany army that had invaded 2,500 km from the border, now had to retreat to the gates of Berlin. The Allied forces which crossed over the Rhine River last month, stormed into the center part of Germany and united with the Russian army. The great combined force, which was joined together last week, has reached and occupied Berlin, the capital of Germany, the city in which the Nazi Empire plotted to conquer the world.

Unauthorized Peek

As we moved toward Japan, Lingayen, on the island of Luzon, was the last and northernmost Philippine airfield to be liberated. From our perspective, we could assume that the airspace over Luzon was finally free of enemy planes and we had an available airfield 100 miles closer to Okinawa. Over the Pacific, the shorter the distance between two islands the safer one felt, for the chance of running out of fuel was far less, and somehow it just seemed better to be able to see land more frequently.

The push to the north increased as we moved all manner of personnel and equipment into Okinawa. One load consisted of paratroopers who begged to be allowed to jump as we approached Naha, Okinawa. Their reason? None had ever landed in an airplane, and they were not sure that it would be safe to descend by any other method than by parachute. During that move north, the whole 11th Airborne Division learned otherwise, for all Troop Carrier

Groups, supplemented by B-24s of several Bomber Groups, were used to ferry the paratroopers from the Philippines to Okinawa. We heard later that the paratroopers felt more comfortable flying with Troop Carrier pilots than with bomber pilots.

Another plane load consisted of 35 nurses and Red Cross women, all of whom had just arrived from the States, plus five tons of condoms! By regulation, we were not permitted to change islands without at least two condoms in our possession, and the MPs often met our flights to check. In addition, two condoms were routinely employed to cover our holstered .45s, to protect the weapon from moisture. With the long flight to Okinawa, the women were bored, and they became curious as to the content of the unmarked cartons. When they asked the crew chief, to avoid embarrassment he said it was classified. A paratroop passenger overheard, and, knowing what the cartons contained, continued to encourage their curiosity; he even offered the use of his jump knife. One of the more adventuresome women slit a box on top of the pile and was deluged by a tide of condoms, which spilled out to cover the cabin floor. In the cockpit we had a good laugh when the crew chief reported the incident and the embarrassment displayed by the curious new arrivals. In the cabin on landing, he was stern, severe, and serious as he proclaimed, "No one gets off till they clean up this mess and repack that carton." So much for an introduction to the war zone.

As the Okinawa campaign heated up, we used the Lingayen airfield more and more, both day and night. Sometime in the interim, an Army field hospital moved in and set up so that our left-hand traffic pattern was directly over their installation. Almost immediately complaints began to funnel in to Squadron, Group, then to 5th Air Force Headquarters, about the noise we made going and coming. (This may have been the very first instance of a noise abatement movement in the history of aviation!) At the time, we who ruled the skies were not about to take flight directions from groundpounders. They could put their hospital anywhere, but the use of this field cut off over 200 air miles to Okinawa for each round trip, and, besides, we had been there first. It was time to strike back!

One of the guys had a friend at Clark who flew a helicopter and who owed him. At that time, the helicopter was just entering the military inventory, and most of us had yet to even see one. And even after we saw one in flight, no one believed that they were safe. To pay off his debt, the helicopter pilot came from Okinawa to Lingayen, right to the hospital, and set down in the middle of the nurses' open-air showers. Our conspirator reported that there were squeals and screams and running in all directions as over two dozen women simultaneously scrambled for towels. He tipped his hat to all and held up a sign:

SALUTATIONS FROM THOSE WHO FLY!

Official reprimands from 5th Air Force Headquarters eventually went out to all who might have been guilty of this indiscretion, but because no one in the area, least of all Troop Carrier, had helicopters, the mystery of the interloper was never solved. However, the hospital no longer complained about the noise of over-flights. And typical of headquarters efficiency, the reprimands didn't even show up until weeks later. By then we were on Ie Shima and could have cared less.

At about this time, I wrote home to my mother.

> 25 July, 1945 Luzon, P.I.
>
> Dear Mom,
>
> Seems I'm always apologizing for not writing often enough. Had 2 letters from you since I wrote last. One of them, a V-Mail was dated 26th March so you can see V-Mail isn't worth a damn especially on a change of address.
>
> Have to fly later this afternoon but I have time for a short letter.
>
> Had to sign a statement today showing preference for staying in the regular Army, Reserve status, active duty or periodic training, subject to call in emergency. Naturally, I chose the last. It may mean a couple of weeks flying a year to keep in practice but that's not too bad.
>
> Mail from Bert hasn't been coming through lately. Seems the mails are all screwed up.
>
> *— censored —*
>
> . . . things ride for a while as long as they keep going smoothly.
>
> Bert's box hasn't come yet but that's understandable. Some of the fellows are still getting Xmas packages. . . .
>
> There is every indication that this war will be over fairly soon. You can't see Okinawa for airstrips and if you could see the hundreds of planes constantly taking off for Japan it would boost your morale 100%. I fully expect to be home at least by this time next year though I doubt it will take that long.
>
> Well have to fly so must leave. Did Bert tell you about Harry

Conover [*creator of a prestigious modeling agency whom she had met while on a buying trip to New York*] praising her figure? Looks like I married a beauty.

Love,
Bob

Incidents: Ground
Naha, Okinawa

There was a time when I was assigned as armed escort officer for two nurses newly arrived at Naha, Okinawa. As our jeep came around a curve, two Marines stepped out from behind thick brush. Not sure of our location, I opted to stop and ask directions. As I approached, it was apparent that these two had been on the line for some time. They were unshaven and covered with dried mud. In fact, the only things clean were their rifles. These living examples of Bill Mauldin's "Willy & Joe" cartoon were staring intently at the nurses. Before I could say anything, one of them asked, "Lieutenant, is that women? American women? I nodded, and the other said, "Can we look at 'em?"

I replied that we could do better than that, and I would bring them over to be introduced. Both of these combat-seasoned veterans reacted with what could only be described as fear as one said, " Oh, no, Lieutenant! We wouldn't know what to say. We ain't even seen a white woman in two years. Just let us stand here and look at them."

At that moment the nurses stepped out of the jeep and started walking toward us. Both Marines turned and fled into the bush. Considering their record of battle on Okinawa, this was probably the only Marine retreat that occurred on that island.

While on duty flying to Okinawa, I heard that a high school classmate was stationed there. The next time I landed there, I called to arrange a meeting. He offered to pick me up in his jeep for a trip to his unit's Officer's Club. By the time we were on the way, it was quite dark, and we were speeding along what was a perfect, brand-new six-lane highway, exchanging information on the home town.

Suddenly, I had a feeling — I guess you could call it a premonition, whatever. I said, "Stop! Right Now!"

My command was so abrupt that he hit the brakes immediately, even though we were traveling fast, burning rubber. Later, he told me that he first thought he was dealing with a case of combat fatigue. But at the time he just decided to humor me by following me up the road as I walked forward in the headlight beams. No more than 300 yards ahead, the road just disappeared, ending in a sheer drop-off. The moon was bright enough to illuminate the bottom, at least 150 feet down. We turned around and went to his unit by his original route, rather than try any new "short cut."

Why such a circumstance? A road that spectacular, ending in the middle of nowhere, and without any warning signs? As the story goes, on the day that Curtis LeMay had arrived, bringing the 21st Air Force's B-29 Superfortresses for the final assault on Japan, as he flew over the island, he asked what all those construction crews were doing. When told that they were building roads, he had one of his legendary outbursts, "The hell with the roads, build runways!"

Incidents: Ground
Location — ?
July-August 1945

The question mark is because I can't remember where this happened. Although it probably was Iwo Jima, it could have been on Okinawa. After a time, all of the islands seemed the same, as we moved almost daily. Mobility was routine for the Troop Carrier Squadron, and the group designation of "Frontline Airline" well defined our role.

One particular time, we were frying bacon, which we had scrounged from tank rations — the only edible food in that assortment. Our culinary activity as usual took place under one of the wings of our plane, which was parked on what in the civilian world would be called the flight line. Dust began to blow onto our bacon from the prop wash of a plane designated by one of the crew immediately as "one big mother." It taxied past us and then past the revetment, where it clearly had intended to park, as indicated by the line chief waving his wands.

Flying planes takes time to learn, and so does taxiing, but taxiing is not nearly as demanding a skill. The fact that this new arrival was apparently over-shooting brought comments, by no means favorable, from nearly everyone within earshot. Then we were all surprised because the "big mother" began backing up. Never had any of us seen a plane back up, and we hurried to investigate. There were four engines; two were shut down but one on each wing was turning a four-bladed prop in reversible pitch as the ship moved backward. Though we had never heard of it, we were face to face with a B-32.

Jane in *Jane's All the World's Aircraft* describes the B-32 Dominator as Consolidated's attempt to expand on the design of its B-24 in order to produce a competitor for Boeing's B-29. The familiar twin tail of the Liberator was replaced with a large single fin and rudder. The development seemingly took much longer than anticipated, and only 114 were built. Four Wright R 3350 engines (2,200 hp) powered the B-32 with Curtiss Electric reversible-pitch four-blade props. Armed with ten .50-caliber machine-guns, it carried 20,000 pounds of bombs. In contrast to the B-29, the B-32 had no pressurization and no remote gun control. The Dominator was the last heavy bomber type to go into action in World War II, but flew only a very few sorties before the Japanese surrender.

As we approached the giant aircraft, ambulances began arriving. Soon bodies were being lifted out of the plane. There was a lot of blood and only some of the crew were alive. The fuselage was punctured fore and aft with bullet holes, and there was a section of the rudder missing. After we helped load the ambulances, we were left alone with the crew chief, who was trying to extract a cigarette from a pack soaked, as was his flight suit, with the blood of his crew. From the master sergeant's service stripes, I could tell he'd been in the Air Corps for some time. As I passed him a lighted cigarette, he told us,

> I got fifty missions over Germany in a -17 and fifty missions over Italy in a -24, but this is my first and last mission over Japan in this bastard. The damn thing's too big and the guns won't cover all sectors. Zeros were coming at us from the blind spots where we couldn't get a shot and just chewing the hell out of us. It got worse when too many of the gunners were hit. I don't know what happened to the other planes in our flight, but we headed here as the closest field.

I heard later that B-32s had covered a paratrooper drop in the Philippines, which was a milk run, but it still would have been a new and puzzling addition to Troop Carrier tactics.

There was also a time when a B-29 landed wheels up and went sliding down the runway to come to a stop off to one side. Because -29s were not based at this field, we assumed that it had been crippled by enemy fire and had headed for the nearest safe haven.

Red flares had preceded the touchdown, and the ambulances chasing the crash vehicles were all too familiar signs that some of the crew had been critically wounded.

Our assumption of combat casualties appeared to be confirmed as medics began removing the bodies of the crew. We counted as we approached the plane, and by calculation, it seemed that everyone was being taken out by stretcher, the majority with faces completely covered.

With so many of the crew decimated, we expected to find the fuselage punctured with multiple holes, but there were none. Not one hole was visible as we walked completely around the plane.

We headed for Operations to find a solution to the mystery. The answer, which had already resulted in several deaths of this crew, was botulism contracted from a contaminated can of chicken. It had been passed around as part of a lunch snack on the long flight to the target. Those still alive were in critical condition, though the copilot had remained functional long enough to get the -29 back on the ground.

We never did learn whether anyone survived, but we were told that the bombing mission had been completed before any of the crew succumbed en route home.

Chapter 10

Toward Surrender

As the summer of 1945 wound down, activity increased and rumors multiplied. We began to hear of plans to invade Japan proper. All of the 11th Airborne had been moved forward to Okinawa from the Philippines, which seemed certain to be the takeoff point for a move into the main islands. Kyushu and Shikoku were thought to be better candidates than Honshu, but where we would land first was only speculation. What was certain was the nature of the opposition that we would encounter. From our point of view in Troop Carrier, dropping paratroopers and gliders was expected to be a formidable task.

Despite the kamikaze attacks on the Fleet at Okinawa, the enemy had held back substantial numbers of planes and pilots to protect the homeland. Troop Carrier formations would be sitting ducks for determined fighter attacks, especially if the attacking pilots cared little whether they themselves survived. Our fighter cover could not be expected to get every Zero flown by Japan's most experienced pilots before we took some losses.

Japan is limited in territory, but not in population. Almost every square yard has people living on it. There would be no such thing as a free drop zone. In the European theater, where troopers were dropped into populated areas, losses were excessive. In Japan, the code of Bushido, which was the ethical standard by which they lived, and the model of the Samurai characterized the culture. Not only would the people be defending their own homes, but they would also be dying for the Emperor, something that was ingrained. We had seen their commanders commit *hara-kiri* as we moved up the island chain, while whole families jumped off cliffs on Okinawa rather than surrender. Daily, wherever we landed, Marines and GIs still flushed Japanese soldiers from caves with flame-throwers and fire fights. Invaders would face not only organized resistance, but every individual could be expected to engage in guerrilla warfare. An enemy willing to fight to the death on his own territory, even if armed with only a pitchfork, was a formidable adversary.

We knew we would have to establish a foothold by air, and the conservative estimate was a 30 percent loss of planes before we could put an effective fighting force on the ground. Our naval forces would be subjected to kamikaze attacks by the several hundred Japanese planes still in readiness for defense. In addition, a new version of the V rocket used by Germany was available — a rocket-powered, piloted, kamikaze attack weapon, dubbed the *Baka bomb*. Baka translates in English as "fool" or "idiot."

If we invaded Japan, estimates of Allied casualties were in excess of a million. And so we waited and wondered, all the time bringing more of everything from the Philippines to Okinawa. On every airstrip, we competed for elbow room with the bombers and fighters that launched constantly, bringing the air war to Japan. And accidents happened.

Three P-51s took off in trail with full bomb racks. The lead either pulled his gear up too quickly or had a malfunction such that the gear collapsed just before he cleared the runway. Whichever, his bombs exploded as his plane refused to fly. The blast got number two, and he went cartwheeling off into the ocean. Number three flew through the smoke and made it. In contrast to steel-matted runways in the southern islands, the Okinawa strip was crushed coral. One bulldozer scraped the debris from the P-51s to the side, while another smoothed the area after a high loader dumped more crushed coral to fill the hole. In less than 15 minutes, we were given clearance for takeoff with the message, "Army -46 in number one position, clear to go. Expedite, we have P-51 squadron on strike profile, waiting to take off."

On one trip from Lingayen to Okinawa, as we passed northeast of Formosa (now Taiwan), we spotted what appeared to be a C-47 headed south. Although C-47s were common farther south, from the Philippines north, the C-46 dominated the transport scene. I turned toward the -47 for a

This, along with other messages, fell from the sky: NAZIS ANNIHILATED!!

ナチドイツ降る

昭和十四年八月に始まったヨーロッパ戰は遂に了った。北はノールウェイ南はエジプト、西はフランス東はスターリングラードに迄達したナチの侵略も反ナチの力のまへに潰えナチの暴力政治はこゝに止んだ。無理は永つゞきしない、必ず失敗する。戰爭を容易い事の樣に考へてポーランド攻略を企てたナチは自國民を始め其侵略の鋒先を向けたヨーロッパ諸國民に有史以來未曾有の破壞と慘めさをもたらしたナチ領袖とそのこれに諂ふ取巻さへなかったなら今回の戰爭はなかったものでしかも戰不利と見るや其暴力政治を強化、宣傳又宣傳で自國民を欺き聯合國側による所罰の自己の身邊に及ぶを恐れて早く降る方戰略的に見て自國に有利なるにも拘らず戰爭を永引かせた。しかし今やヨーロッパに平和は來たドイツの再建も俘虜となっても生存へて居た其一百万をこゆる人達の力で大に早められよう。更生も出來よう。今や勝って驕らざる反ナチの總軍力は東の方日本軍部の打倒に向ふものである。

See bottom of next page for translation.

better look, in hopes of identifying the new group that might be entering our territory. It dove for the water, as the only defensive maneuver available to an unarmed transport. As I crossed above him, I could see his wings emblazoned with big red meatballs that indicated his affiliation with the air force of the empire of Japan. I had encountered their copy of our DC-3. He, without guns; I, without guns. I waved at him; he waved back — two ships that passed over the Philippine Sea.

After Germany surrendered, we showered Japan with leaflets warning them of their similar fate. Our "psych" warfare people gave it their best, but they didn't believe that words would do the job — not when Japanese soldiers kept crawling out of the caves and holes in the ground in "secure" areas with the intent of trying to do us bodily harm.

Rumors continued to fly. Contradictory messages came in simultaneously. We heard about "The Bomb" and maybe a second one, so awesome in explosive power that the war would most assuredly end. Meanwhile, we were briefed to search en route for the cruiser *Indianapolis*, which was missing and believed sunk after departing from Tinian for the Philippines. In retrospect, the two events were related, because the *Indianapolis* had transported the bomb to the Pacific. Ironically, it had off-loaded before being sunk by a submarine on the next leg of its journey.

On Ie Shima I sat in the entrances of the burial crypts that surrounded the bay and watched the Japanese suicidal assault on the Fleet. I was sleeping on a canvas cot under the wing of a C-46, when one Zero with bomb attached went through the wing of a parked neighbor. The bomb was a dud,

---

The reverse side of the Nazis Annihilated!! propaganda piece (previous page) stated:

THE NAZIS HAVE SURRENDERED

World War II, which began in the fourteenth year of Showa (1939), has at last come to an end. The Nazis, whose armed aggression reached as far north as Norway, as far south as Egypt, as far west as France, and as far east as Stalingrad, have been destroyed. Those opposed to the Nazis have put an end to this violent regime. Such regimes cannot last; they must always fail. The Nazis thought war an easy endeavor and planned the conquest of Poland. The Nazis caused suffering unparalleled in history to be visited on their own country, and the countries of Europe they tried to invade. If Hitler and the group of sycophants around him had not existed, there would have been no war. When they realized they were losing the war, they made their violent regime even more violent. They deceived their own people with propaganda. Thinking about the punishment they would receive from the Allied Powers, they prolonged the war, though it would have been strategically advantageous to surrender. But now peace has come to Europe. The reconstruction of Germany will be greatly hastened by the strength of the more than one million people who survived even though they became prisoners of war. The prisoners will be able to become part of society. The Allied Powers are without arrogance even though they have defeated the Nazis, but they will head east to defeat the Japanese military.

so the results were one dead pilot, one totaled C-46, and one trophy — a ceremonial sword. That same attack was followed by another, which prompted my navigator to start running toward a foxhole behind a line of parked P-61 Black Widows. This time the bomb exploded resulting in three destroyed P-61s and a chagrined lieutenant who had been running right at the point of explosion, which knocked him down but left him uninjured. Because these attacks were uncoordinated and were often made by pilots who scarcely knew how to control their planes, the points of contact were random, quite unpredictable.

6 August 1945 — *Enola Gay* drops *Little Boy* on Hiroshima
9 August 1945 — *Big Boy* dropped on Nagasaki
10 August 1945 — Japanese envoys report to General MacArthur in the Philippines to be informed of the terms and logistics of the surrender
14 August 1945 — Emperor Hirohito assembles the Supreme Council and accepts unconditional surrender.

Then there was confirmation.

After Hiroshima and Nagasaki, the Japanese gave up. On Ie Shima, every gun seemed to go off at once. We ran for the burial crypts to escape the shrapnel that started falling like rain. Although there was no official report, I would guess that some of our last casualties in the Pacific were the result of celebration.

After things calmed down, we still wondered if it was really over, as did many soldiers and sailors throughout the Pacific. Our reassurance came before others', for we were on Ie Shima when the white Japanese Betty bomber with green crosses on its wings and tail entered the traffic pattern. Months before, on airfields in the south, we had become quite familiar with the sound of the twin-engine Betty, for either there was no mechanism to synchronize the engines or the pilots were indifferent to the asynchronous beats. The sound was unnerving to any multi-engine pilot, and implied a lack of respect for the aircraft — no cadet would have been allowed to fly with engines out of sync.

The Betty landed and was directed to a parking area. Military Police were there, but so were hundreds of GIs, each with his own gun. Before them were the representatives of a nation that had attempted to kill them just days

Photos *A-F*: The special Japanese Betty stopped at Ie Shima to refuel on the way to the Philippines for the meeting with General Douglas MacArthur.

before. As the Japanese exited the plane, they seemed chagrined, an expected reaction for a people who rely so much on saving face. The officers carried Samurai swords and side arms. There was no ceremony — everyone just waited for the plane to be refueled and towed to takeoff position for the last leg of the journey to meet with General Douglas MacArthur in the Philippines to agree to the preliminary surrender terms. GIs, curious to a

fault, said little, but they lined the runway to watch the Betty depart, its props still amazingly beating the air.

Since that time, there have been many opinions about the employment of the atomic bomb. No one that I met in that environment ever for a moment felt that the use of the bomb in that context was improper. Many of us, after seeing too many good men die, had developed a fondness for the idea of continuing to live. If Harry Truman hadn't decided to use the bomb, over one million more of us, plus probably two million Japanese, might not have survived.

The tradeoff was the 200,000 lives lost in Hiroshima and Nagasaki. I visited those cities weeks after the bombing and saw the devastation, which was no worse than that produced by the high explosives and incendiaries dropped on Tokyo and Yokohama. The factor hardest to incorporate was that only one bomb produced so much destruction.

Those who have been in combat learn a cruel lesson: There is no nice way to die in war. Those who have not seen combat should not be surprised to find that their opinions on military matters tend to be discounted, for they are hardly qualified to comment, when they have had no such personal experience.

My letters home around this time showed relief at a resolution and a primary concern with getting home.

15 August 1945
Luzon, Philippine Islands

Dear Mom,

Well it looks like it's finished at last; but unfortunately that doesn't mean I can come dashing right home. We've been on pins and needles for the last three days all with the expectation of seeing Japan in practically the first wave. Well though it was an [*accepted*] thing by everyone, tonight the whole thing fizzled so we may take a long time to fly over the Emperor's palace and the orders may change again at a moment's notice. It really makes very little difference now that the whole thing is over. Everyone is naturally only interested in going home as soon as possible. As far as we know no orders have been given of any change from the 900 hours and 14 months before we can go home. Even so there will undoubtedly be a change. Of course I'll let you know as soon as I do.

It's late now and the lights are about to go out. Will write rest tomorrow.

And now tomorrow and so far as it appears anyway the war might not be over for we are just following the same routine as we have for months. With one exception they seem to think we can get more time by flying nights. Now that the war is over there's no need to rush anything and as is natural everyone is bitching for they all believe and rightly too that with the exception of personnel there is no load worth taking by plane considering the cost. They've got lots of time and boats don't have to worry about weather.

I suppose it's natural with everyone interested in getting home. The opinion of the fellows in general is most of us who have been over six months or more will be home for Christmas. Another idea is that pilots who have from 50-60 discharge points. I have 55 now and [*am*] getting them at the rate of 2/month with a possible five for another campaign star.

I realize I haven't written in quite some time, but we have been busy preparing the way for occupation. I expect in a few days censorship will be lifted and so in your next letter you can ask all those things I couldn't tell you before and as soon as it's OK you'll get the answers. . . .

I hope Mom it won't be too long now before I'm home again. I intend getting there as fast as the airlines can travel as soon as I hit the States which unfortunately may not be for some time to come.

It's time for dinner even if it is only bully beef and dehydrated potatoes. Boy what I wouldn't give for some cold milk and fresh vegetables.

Will write again soon. Be seeing you.

Love,
Bob

22 August 1945
Luzon, Philippine Islands

Dear Mom,

Rain has made us rather inactive so I find time to write to you. Just got a letter from you telling of the effect of the news at home. I wrote all about that to Bert and if she hasn't showed it to you ask her to let you see that part.

The big effect over here was that we started to work and fly like the devil, night and day and it hasn't stopped yet. We have no more shack and we are living out of B-4 bags, ready to jump. I've no doubt I'll be seeing Japan before long. By the time you get this you'll probably have read all about it in the papers.

Of course we have just the same amount of rumors. When censorship is lifted I'll be able to tell you a lot of interesting facts. Traveling around you can amass a lot of information. I saw the Japs come in from Japan the other day but you've heard all about that.

Haven't any way of telling when I can come home but there's every indication it will be sooner than we at first expected. They may use points to send us home. I have about 55-60 now and of course it will be lowered. There are plenty of replacements if they send them. Troop Carrier and Air Transport Command are the ones who'll have to do all the work now.

I'm looking forward to seeing Jack H. [*a boyhood chum, who had received a battlefield commission, Silver Star, and Purple*

Heart on a recon mission, which involved swimming the Rhine with vital information, despite a machine-gun bullet in the head].

The radio just said, "waves and waves of transports will drop the first occupation paratroops all over Japan." Need I say more?

Bert sent me some snaps of herself. Quite an improvement I think. Very, Very nice. You should hear the fellows exclaim over them, especially the bathing suit ones.

There was something I put in one of my letters that happened here and before I mailed it an order came from the censor saying not to mention it so I cut it out myself. [*This was probably the sinking of the cruiser* ***Indianapolis***.]

Glad Jack made lieutenant. He deserves it and since he is about the only one of the gang who wasn't an officer, I know it hurt his pride. I'm proud of all my friends. They certainly showed that they all have what it takes.

Will write more maybe from Japan next time when I find time. Write when you can.

Love,
Bob

Chapter 11

Occupation

A short while after the Betty bomber had stopped to refuel, in mid-August 1945, we were dispatched to Iwo Jima to fly daily shuttles of 50-gallon drums of aviation gas to Atsugi Air Base, Japan. The fuel was needed for return trips, as the Air Corps began to bring in the occupation forces. So it was that we landed early on our first day in a country full of people who had been trying to kill us for four years. Rumor was that there were still quite a few Japanese intent on doing us harm. That day, on the airfield, there was just us and work crews to unload and fuel the planes — no extra troops, not even MPs. They would appear with the paratroops we would bring in the following week. Until these troopers arrived with their Military Police, there was a sort of civil hiatus during which it was unclear whether anyone was responsible for anything.

Curious, and with time to spare that first day, I invited my crew chief to join me for a look around. He armed himself with a Thompson submachine-gun, much more formidable than my .45 side arm. We walked toward what had appeared to be a small village just a few hundred yards from the airfield.

First, we came to a small farmhouse set back from the road, surrounded by a grove of trees. No adults were visible, but a small child of about two was sitting in the front yard, crying. He held on to a little toy truck, which was minus a wheel. Initially, I thought that the missing wheel was the cause of his tears, but in the process of replacing it for him, I realized that he had been abandoned by the adults, who had fled inside the house when they saw us coming up the road. Obviously, they were not going to come to his rescue while we were present. This, in itself was sufficient reason to push on.

Just a bit farther on, we came to the main street of the little village. There was no one in sight. Shutters were over the windows and garden gates were closed. We walked along the deserted street until we came to one of the larger buildings with a front porch, covered with little shoes all neatly arranged in rows. It had to be the school; and in we went.

I opened the door, walked through a small foyer, and came to a large room, which appeared to be the main office. Several women at desks in the back of the room looked up in fear, but no one moved. In the center of the room, and just in front of me, a man was absorbed in writing something, apparently unaware of our presence. Not daring to trust what Japanese I had learned from the manual distributed to all combat troops, I rapped on his desk with my knuckle.

He looked up, and in perfect English said, “Good morning, Lieutenant. I wondered how long it would take you to get here.”

I was completely surprised by his use of my language and said so. He laughed and attributed his skill to a Master’s degree in English from Columbia University. He seemed relieved that we were finally in his country, for as he reported, the two previous weeks had been nothing but constant aerial attacks by every type of plane of both the U.S. Army and the Navy. Some, he said, even dropped empty coke bottles, whose whine as they fell was quite unnerving. I asked if we could see some of the children, and he readily agreed. He warned us that initially they would be afraid after years of exposure to the propaganda, which had claimed that we were truly devils, interested only in maiming and raping, especially if we wore the accursed silver wings. His description even frightened me. He added that they needed to learn that it was otherwise and what better place to start than in a school. We left our guns on his desk and went to meet the students in the equivalent of our fifth grade.

As we walked into the classroom, all of the children looked petrified. The principal made what sounded like reassuring remarks, then introduced us. Their facial expressions were solemn until the sergeant wrote the answers to their arithmetic homework problems on the blackboard. I had an inspiration

Mt. Fuji touching the clouds, elevation, 12,388 feet.

and suggested that the occasion of our arrival should be a day off from school. The principal made the announcement, and everyone smiled. They grabbed their books and ran out laughing and chattering like children have a right to.

After more conversation and the promise to meet with him at our next opportunity, we picked up our guns and left the school to find the street full of the townspeople. I sent the sergeant back for the principal to act as our interpreter. He smilingly informed us that the children had run home to report that we were not devils. He laughed as he claimed that the only problem was that both the mayor and the police chief were arguing over who would have the privilege of being the first to serve us tea. I proposed neutral ground, and they both contributed to a tea in the principal's office. He suggested that I consider becoming a diplomat rather than piloting planes, for my suggestion had defused an ongoing political struggle for power between the two august Japanese gentlemen.

We got back to the field just in time to take off for another round trip — this time to prepare for bringing in the paratroops. I decided on that day that I would be willing to invade any country any time, if I could be sure that the children's fears would turn to laughter and all could have a holiday.

Incidents: Air
August 1945

In retrospect, the highlight of the aerial approach to Atsugi had been the view of Mt. Fuji. With an elevation of over 12,000 feet, Fuji was our first sighting of the Empire of Japan. Though at the time I was not given to taking pictures, this initial view demanded recording. As we got closer, the urge to see into the crater resulted in another photo.

In subsequent months, I visited inns in the foothills around this mountain and had the opportunity to view it from many perspectives. Mt. Fuji has a mystical, magnetic quality, ever stable, yet ever changing. It is easy to see how this mountain figured in the culture and religion of the Japanese people.

In flight, Mt. Fuji serves as a checkpoint, more compelling than any beacon. On the ground, there are times when Mt. Fuji does seem to touch the face of God. Over 40 years later, while visiting my son, who at the time was a fighter weapons instructor at Nellis AFB, Nevada, I was drawn to a color photo on his living room wall. It was a picture of his F-4, beautifully silhouetted against the snow-capped peak of Mt. Fuji. His comment: "Dad, you just have to fly over Fuji to appreciate its beauty." Perhaps it is true: The more things change, the more they stay the same.

28 August 1945 — USS *Missouri* sails into Tokyo Bay to accept the surrender. 4th Marines land at Yokosuka.
30 August 1945 — 11th Airborne arrives at Atsugi.
2 September 1945 — Surrender ceremony aboard the *Missouri*.

[*Destinations are not listed in my Form 5, but daily flight times exceeding six hours occurred on 13, 14, 18, 19, 25, 26, 30, and 31 August.*]

1 September 1945 Iwo Jima

Dear Mom,

Well now I can tell you most everything so that ought to please you since some of the questions you asked previously looked as if they were drafted in Tokyo.

Of course with the radio you probably know more about what I'm doing than I do.

You can see the reason for our recent move was to get us nearer Tokyo. In line with that I've already made one flight into Atsugi (Tokyo-Yokohama airdrome) right behind MacArthur incidentally. Of course we couldn't go far from the field but I did meet several of the Jap military and a few civilians. . . . They salute and bow all over the place and seem to be working hard to please. We are flying in equipment for the 11th Airborne you hear so much about on the radio.

I'm writing Bert and rather than write it twice ask her to let you read those comments on the occupation. It's very hard to write for all we have is a bunk and I must write lying down.

I imagine this place is only temporary and all rumors have it that we will move to one of the larger airdromes outside a large city in Japan and fly within the country itself.

When the first reports of the surrender came through I was on Clark Field P.I. and we were immediately alerted for occupation

The view of Mt. Fuji through the pilot's windshield.

The Mt. Fuji crater, taken at 13,000 feet.

and began flying the equipment and men of the 11th Airborne to Okinawa night and day for a week, expecting each day to take off for Japan.

As for staying over here nothing has been said to change the 14 months and 900 hours, but we expect to be home much sooner than that. It's a safe bet to say that Troop Carrier will be the last of the Air Corps to go home.

As soon as I know anything definite, I'll tell you.

The attendance at church on the 15th was practically 100% over here.

I believe I will get another battle star for Okinawa and that means 5 more points. I now have about 60, which should be enough to get out when I do get home. Battle stars are given for participating in campaigns and flying over enemy occupied territory. Just because a C-46 doesn't carry guns doesn't mean it never gets in exciting situations, like trying to decide whether to plow through a thunderhead or take a chance of Jap fighters and go over Formosa to circle it.

I doubt if Bill will have to come over. They don't need fighters anymore. All that branch or almost all expect to go home soon.

Well, I've seen both Tokyo and Yokohama so I'm ready to go home any time they'll let me.

Will write more later. All my mail will go to the original APO as I don't expect to be here long.

Love,
Bob

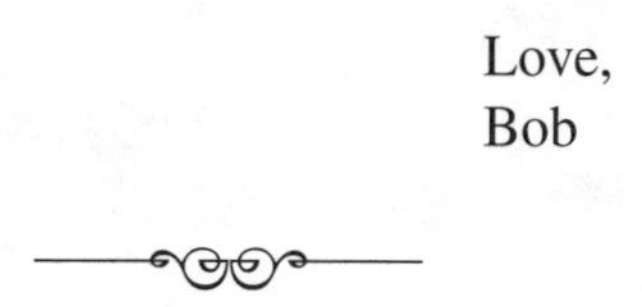

Engineer Duty

I don't remember whether it was on the second or third day at Atsugi that our turn-around time was extended for reasons that no one ever bothered to explain. Before noon we were told that our takeoff for return to Iwo would not be until after sunset. This gave us a whole afternoon of free time, the first in weeks. Someone came up with the thought, "Why don't we go to Tokyo?"

I got out the aerial map, which indicated that Atsugi was not that far from Tokyo and Yokohama. But we had no wheels. None of our vehicles had arrived yet, and the Japanese vehicles on the field, which were coal burners, didn't look like they could make the distance, even if we could get them started. The map showed that a railroad ran right by Atsugi and straight into the heart of Tokyo. All we had to do was catch the train.

At the time, and I'm sure it is still the case, the people depended almost completely on rail transport. An electrically powered engine pulled anywhere from three to six coaches at quite a respectable speed. In our experience, it was as if the New York subway system had been copied, with the difference that these trains ran above ground. Despite inflicting extensive destruction to Japanese military installations, our bombing and strafing attacks apparently had been planned to leave the railroads intact. Although square-mile areas in Tokyo and Yokohama were completely flattened, the only burned-out rolling stock that I saw were streetcars in the cities, and these had been strafed by fighters.

As we walked the short distance to the rail line, it seemed that trains were going east about every 15 minutes. There was no station platform anywhere within sight, so we stood by the track with the intent of waving down the next approaching train. The first went by, and 15 minutes later the second even speeded up when the engineer spotted the five of us trying to get him to stop. As Einstein said, "What can the fish know about the water he swims in?" In retrospect, having just invaded the day before, we undoubtedly looked pretty ominous to all Japanese. Of course, our image wasn't helped by the fact that the crew chief and radio man were both carrying submachine-guns, the navigator had a carbine, and the other pilot and I had shoulder-holster .45s.

Our plan didn't seem to be working, and as the third train approached, I opined that this was the last chance. If this one didn't stop, then we were not going to see Tokyo that day. The crew chief, frustrated by our failure, saw this train begin to speed up, and fired a Tommy-gun burst at the train's wheels, producing spectacular flashes as the bullets ricocheted off. But this display was nothing compared to the sparks that flew when the engineer slammed on the brakes, bringing the train to a complete stop. Shades of the old American West!

The doors opened. We had succeeded, and we climbed aboard the first car, which also served as the engine. Everyone inside looked quite uneasy, as our appearance was hardly a routine event in any of their lives, most never having even seen Americans before. However, at the time, our concern was that the train wasn't moving. I went to the front to investigate and found no engineer. Apparently, our method of stopping the train had so frightened him that he had quit on the spot and simply blended in with the passengers. No one came forward, and there we sat.

As a ten-year-old, I had once visited my cousin in Brooklyn, and we had spent an entire day riding, transferring around to every line on the New York subway system, all for five cents apiece. Naturally, we rode in front where we could watch the engineer. I remembered the glamour of the power and the speed, and I even considered becoming an engineer, as dazzled ten-year-olds are wont to do.

Of course, I would never have dared share this childish fantasy with my crew, but I volunteered to become the engineer. Their collective response was, "You think you can do it?"

To which I replied, "I can fly an airplane, so I ought to be able to drive a damn train. You don't even have to steer it. You just make it go and stop."

And it was as simple as I said. My one problem all the way to Tokyo was getting the cars lined up evenly with the station platform at each of the many stops along the way. After our passengers realized that we were really benevolent hijackers, many of the apprehensive looks began to recede. As I pulled into the Tokyo station terminal, the reluctant engineer came forward. We exchanged bows, and I gave him his train back. He said, "*Arrigato*" (thank you).

The Tokyo station rivaled Grand Central in size and was filled with people at that hour. Most looked at us fearfully, but I seemed to be singled out for more of the frightened looks than my colleagues. I was puzzled by this distinction, for while I hadn't expected a welcome with open arms, I couldn't see why I would appear more ominous than those with me who carried submachine-guns. Everywhere we walked, people made way; many bowed, and some looked to be on the verge of fainting. All in all, our odyssey was not proving to be fun. We were scaring people by just being there. We caught the next train west, this time as passengers. With sign language and pointing to the train controls at the appropriate time, I managed to get the train to stop when we reached Atsugi.

After another round-trip flight to Iwo, I had time to visit again with the local school principal whom I had met on the first day. I reviewed the details of our excursion to Tokyo and inquired as to the reason why I seemed to stimulate more fear in the populace than my companions. I had remembered his statements from the first meeting, when he told me that the people particularly feared those who wore wings. But that could not have accounted for the difference in the Tokyo station, because we all wore them.

He asked, "Were you wearing that jacket in Tokyo? If so, it was because of the kiri leaf."

His reference was to the Group insignia emblazoned on my field jacket.

The emblem was in the shape of a leaf on which was written in Japanese, "The kiri leaf has fallen." I knew that this phrase referred to a saying from Japanese folklore: "Japan will survive as long as the kiri leaf remains on the tree." It was intended to mean that the Empire would last forever, because the kiri leaf, which is shaped like an oak leaf, stays on the branch even in winter. My friend explained that this phrase was not merely folklore, but was an intrinsic belief, as was the invulnerability of the Japanese Imperial Dynasty in Shinto, the state religion. The reaction to this insignia indicated that the psych warfare boys had scored a coup. I never wore that insignia in Japan again.

In later years, I wondered if the Japanese people's initial reaction to us was solely based on the propaganda to which they had been exposed for four years. Certainly some of their male relatives had returned home on leave during that period from places like Singapore and Manila, where they had been the occupying army. If the truth had been told earlier about the actions of the Japanese military as conquerors, the people would have assumed that an occupation always involves rape and pillage.

12 September 1945
Japan

Dear Mom,

I'm just spending the night here on another trip from Ie Shima. You see we've moved from Iwo Jima and now we are bringing occupation troops from Okinawa and hauling back prisoners of war. I've been awfully busy and have hardly had time to myself. One of your letters came just before I left Iwo and this is the first chance I've had to answer. I'm writing this on the navigator's table in the ship.

Finally got a package from Bert and the T shirts and tobacco come in handy since I'm hardly anywhere long enough to find a PX. Bert's mail has been suffering to but I have managed a few letters on Japan I'm sure you'd be interested in.

As a consequence of this moving the mail is coming in fits and starts, but it's pleasant to be surprised.

Nothing has been said about speeding up the going home

except those with over 85 points. I have only about 60 or 65 which isn't near enough and at the rate of only 2 a month it will take a year. The other possibility is time and hours as it has always been which would mean at least 7 more months here. The flying time in hours would be no problem.

You can see I would welcome some means of getting home for as far as I'm concerned it's only a half year of wasted time that I could be using to good advantage.

The Doc and I have had several talks and he mentioned the numerous fields open in the social as well as the educational set up even with only an MA in psychology. I figure that I could get a BA in 2 years by taking [an] accelerated course and possibly an MA in 3. I certainly intend to try like hell.

Looks like I'm in the hometown paper often. Wait till they get the story of our outfit being in on the first day of the occupation.

Write as often as you can.

Love,
Bob

Incidents: Ground
Tachikawa, Japan

Soon after moving into Tachikawa as home base, I had occasion to meet the local pharmacist, who offered to act as a guide and interpreter. After our first meeting, he sent me the following letter, which indicates how one Japanese citizen felt about the war and the subsequent U.S. military occupation.

To respect & esteem Mr. John

For a long time, I had waiting these days come. I don't like strife. I like peace. And you, too. You came to our country with true peace and freedom. Thanks very much. You are far more kind and gentle than Japanese military man. Indeed, Japanese army force and Japanese officials are savage — no kind, no gentle, moreover, very wilful. They oppressed our poor nation —

1st Lieutenant John R. Lester.

esp. the man who likes peace that is the opponent of the war — and threw us into the war. We were torment for a long time. (During that time I must study English secretly. Because if it was found by Japanese M.P. I shall be punished on suspicion of spy.)

But now they were defeated. Serve them right! At last, our poor nation became free from their chain. Now, I feeling true willing. I am very glad and many thanks to your country on the same time. New Japan was born. Japan returned to our nation. Peace has come.

I think, peace and quiet both are quite necessary for our life. The object of our life is to love and freedom. Peace, freedom and equality are quite important.

Go away, I say — Japanese privileged classes and Japanese military men! Melt away, I say, Japanese rich savage, too! They are all very bad and harmful to us. I say good bye, bad and cruel fellows! My blood boils up with indignation. I shall say more to them.

"Great liar! I should like to knock you down all together!"

10 Oct. '45
at Philosopher's Cottage
Fujitaro Kato

In the same time frame, the following editorial appeared in the Tachikawa Army Air Base paper, *The TAABloid* (vol. II, no. 1).

January 8, 1946

As Time Goes By

So much has been said about the American Way of Life, and the ideals of the Americans, that the other day we started to wonder exactly what mysterious thing causes civilians to turn into soldiers, soldiers into men of mercy, and soldiers who are willing to forgive, and forget . . . . . all too easily.

During the war that slogan, "Uphold the American Way of Life", was a handy little gadget. It was a whole stew of propaganda rolled up in one meat ball, served palatably to soldier and civilian alike. About the most proponderous [*sic*] exponent of the theme was the Nash-Kelvinator Company, who ran weekly ads designed to bring the soldiers home from the foxholes for a few minutes. The result was that the G.I. begot himself the reputation of being a very rugged fellow on the battlefield, but was oh-so-weak emotionally.

Most of the G.I.'s complained about the type of dribble that was turned out about them. But be it dribble or not, it took it's effect. Sub-consciously, the G.I. liked to see his thoughts of home put into print and illustrated so that the folks at home could see what he was going through. And then . . . . slowly and surely, this thing called the American Way of Life became part of every man and woman. According to this new treatise the American was a peacful [*sic*] person, but when someone stepped on his toes he became awfully mad. If someone tortured American prisoners he would never reciprocate because he wanted to show the enemy the "right way". He would go through HELL to win a war; would endure mud, shell-fire, privation heat, and anything else designed to make a man miserable. After winning that war, he would forget and forgive.

Actually, it would be unfair to blame forgiveness entirely on the G.I., because it wasn't his fault. It was simply a case of putting a man on an island for month upon month, removing every bit of civilization, and then, after leading that type of existence sending him in on an Army of Occupation. Even though the people did look queer and the air did have the odor of human dungue [*sic*], it was civilization. There was the excuse. But did the excuse prove strong enough to warrant forgiving and forgetting?

Ask a man who has just come over from stateside, or a man who came here fresh off the Islands. Ask him why he is so friendly to the people who would have given anything in their power to kill him less than five months ago. The answer he will give you is simply this; The war is over, Why stay mad at these people? After all it wasn't their fault.

The war is over . . . . but the crosses and the Stars of David still stand on every island from Guadalcanal to Okinawa. Each cross marks the grave of a man who was no different than you or I. A man who was placed there because one of these friendly Nips put him there.

But yet, the American way goes on. The doctrine of love thy

> neighbor still persists, and the G.I. still cashes in on the good thing by selling cigarettes, to the people who once vowed to kill him. The last war ended in the exact same way . . . . we all know the results. This war is ended . . . . and only time will tell the results. Will historians say that we forgave too easily?
>
> S.S.P. (author unknown)

The above is reprinted *in toto* for a contemporary opinion. After 50 years and more wars, how does the reader answer the last question? Is it obvious?

Incidents: Ground
Tachikawa, Japan

There was a time, after losing our experienced enlisted crews whose point requirements for going home were much lower than ours, when we as pilots had very little to do. I volunteered to help in the infirmary where we handled routine emergencies, referring our people to the base hospital if serious and, per existing regulations, treating our Japanese helpers for whatever. Because the regulations prohibited our physicians from treating Japanese civilians, I had the opportunity to fill this gap at least for the Japanese personnel who worked on the base. Physicians from the base hospital regularly stood by and offered guidance as I learned to suture, treat severe burns, perform skin grafts, and even set bones. To be instrumental in relieving pain was sufficient reason to want to branch out. After all, we had the only medicine available — sulfa and the new miracle drug, penicillin, whose properties were not yet fully understood. I started pushing the idea that we ought to investigate whether we could make a contribution to those confined in a nearby leprosarium. I recruited a nurse and a group of physicians, and took a sample of every medicine that might conceivably have some effect on the condition.

Webster defines leprosy as "a chronic infectious disease of the skin, tissues, or nerves, characterized by ulcers, white scaly scabs, deformities, etc." You have to see it to believe it. My first visual exposure was a shock, and I could certainly understand why lepers have been shunned throughout history. With the physicians' guidance, over a period of time, I tried every medicine that we had. Gentian violet, when applied to open lesions, seemed to have some positive effect in arresting ulcer development. Nothing else seemed to do much good, but the patients were clearly appreciative of our

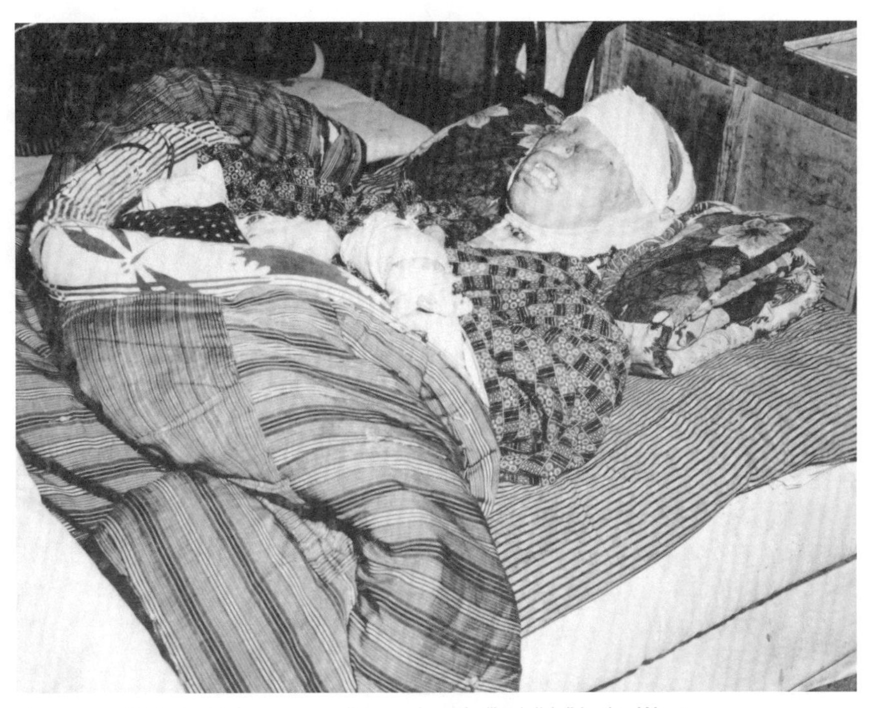

Japanese afflicted with Leprosy, a disease largely "invisible" in the West.

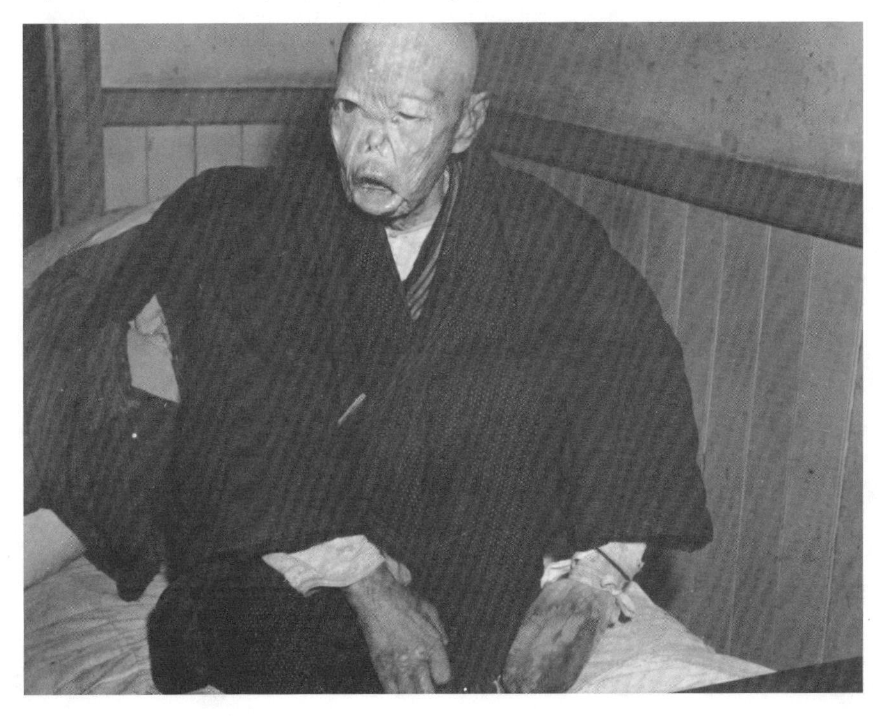

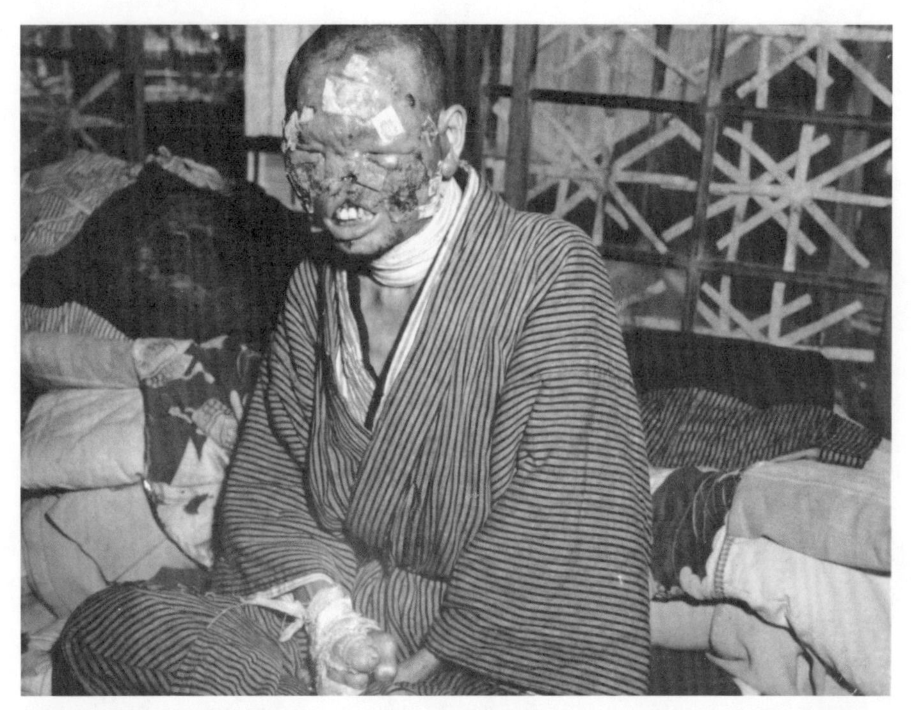

Leprosy.

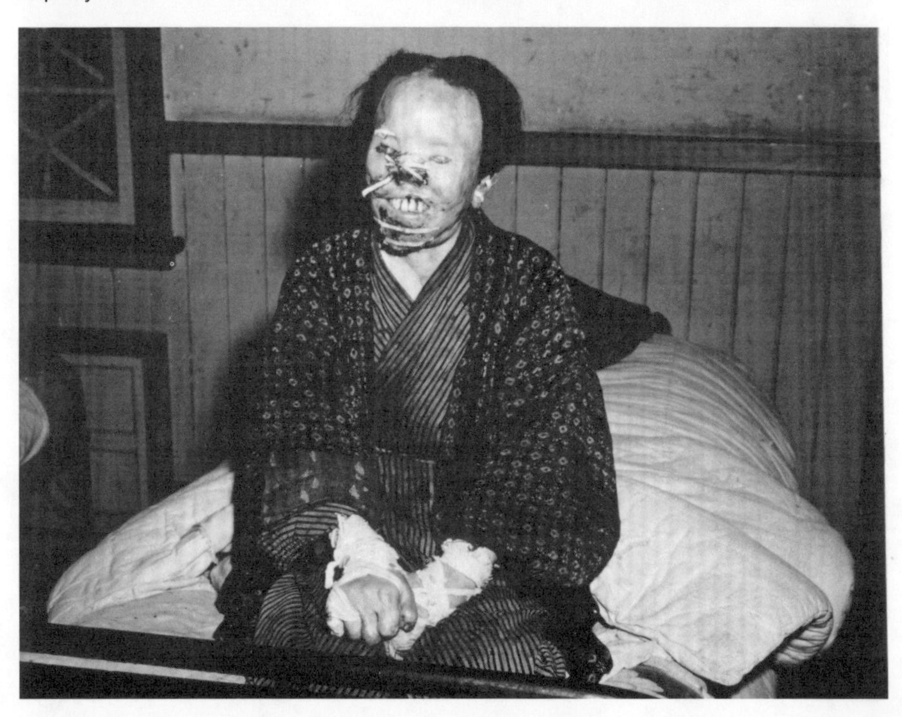

"Chocolate eaters."

efforts. Their attitude of hopelessness was profound, for the condition was terminal.

Tragically, this attitude extended to the entire family, and all, including the children, were incarcerated to await death. I could get candy and toys for the children, and this much we did accomplish. Never again since my sojourn in that leprosarium have I been exposed to so much concentrated misery in one location.

That was in January 1946. Happily, since then, medicine has relieved the misery.

One night at about 0200, I was awakened by a tentative rapping on the infirmary office door. In response to my, "Enter," there appeared a six-foot-plus-sized soldier with fear in his eyes as he contemplated his penis, which was obviously trapped in the neck of a bottle.

"Sir, what I go'na do? If you break it, you're go'na kill me!"

I adopted my most serious expression and agreed that this situation did require special attention, by implication perhaps even a trip to the base hospital. I asked him to accompany me to the jeep. When he turned to go, I took my .45 out of the desk drawer and hid it behind my back. I followed him out into a night that was so silent we could hear the crickets chirping — that is until the two shots from my hidden .45-caliber. The patient was startled; the bottle fell off, to the ground. First, he expressed surprise, then relief, then glee.

"Sir, you'se a genius. You saved my life."

I did suppress the chuckle until my patient departed.

Incidents: Air
Osaka, Japan

The war was over, but as part of the occupation, people and supplies still needed to be moved; and Troop Carrier was the Army's airline. Soon we were familiar with most of the airfields on the islands of Japan. On a bright and sunny day, in early fall 1945 when we called for landing clearance at Osaka, the tower asked if we were equipped for ILS (Instrument Landing System). My "Affirmative" confirmed the presence of a receiver display instrument in my cockpit. Osaka tower asked if I would cooperate by being the first to make an instrument landing using the new ILS equipment, which had just been installed. I agreed, for this would be the first time I had ever had the opportunity to attempt an ILS landing as well, because the field transmitters and trained ground personnel were just then beginning to appear overseas.

The system works thus. One airfield transmitter (the localizer) sends a radio beam along the axis of the runway. Another transmitter beside the runway emits a beam that indicates the glide-slope to that runway. In the cockpit, the pilot maneuvers so that a vertical needle is centered, which keeps the plane lined up with the runway, while the horizontal pointer is aligned with a line on the dial to maintain the correct glide-slope.

I could hardly wait to try this new gadget, but in the "old school," I had been taught not to fully trust directions from ground controllers, slip sticks for load adjustments, or, for that matter, even navigators, without resorting to some personal dead reckoning. To give a fair test, I elected to keep my head down and fly by instruments, but I asked the copilot to keep his eyes open for whatever.

The vertical and horizontal pointers on the ILS dial began to wave at me, and I centered the vertical, which brought a terse "Army C-46 you're on course" from the ground controller. Holding the heading, I set up a rate of descent, which soon led to, "You're right on the glide-slope." Simple and easy, I thought, as I held the heading and the rate of descent, especially when the ground controller came on with the reassuring, "Army C-46, you're A-OK on heading and glide-slope, approaching the middle marker."

At that point, my copilot tapped me on the shoulder, pointed ahead and asked, "Do you think that smokestack that we are about to fly into might scratch our paint?"

I made a 60-degree bank to avoid it — standing all alone right in our glide path, while ground control excitedly informed me that I was going off both the course and the glide-slope.

I responded with, "You damn near directed me into a smokestack."

His reply, hardly regulation, was, "Jesus, they assured me that they had torn that stack down yesterday."

So much for my pioneering effort on ILS, but it would have been a good landing, if it hadn't been for that smokestack.

Incidents: Ground
Tokyo, Japan

Ofttimes in trips to the city, I passed the Daichi building, which was General MacArthur's Headquarters. Always there was a gathering of Japanese citizens in front of this imposing structure, presumably to get a view of their new leader, who for some Japanese had taken the place of the Emperor, at least in terms of the power that affected their lives. It was known that the General came and went at all hours, following no regular pattern. Hence, he might appear at any time of day and enter his automobile, which was always waiting at the front entrance.

On one trip to Tokyo, we were late and had to run if we were to catch the train back to Tachikawa. I must have been in better shape than my companion, for as we sprinted toward the train station, I was almost a half block ahead of him as I approached the Daichi building. Still running, I looked back and shouted to him to speed up. At that point I bumped into someone.

After regaining my balance, I turned to see that the someone was General Douglas MacArthur, who as usual, without any warning, had just exited the building. I saw stars, for there were ten of them, just on his collar tabs alone. I saluted, wondering what the penalty might be for nearly knocking down the Supreme Allied Commander of the Pacific Forces and Administrator of the Empire of Japan.

The General looked at me and said, "Good afternoon, Lieutenant," as he returned the salute with a smile and got into his automobile.

Back at the Air Base, my companion told everyone that General MacArthur and I had had a conversation that day. Technically, I guess that was true.

The Talisman

It was a skull with a top hat, about an inch and a half in length, probably worth no more than 50 cents. I can't remember where I picked it up or even why. I attached it to the zipper on my flight suit before I ever got into a cockpit. It was there when after 7½ hours of flight time in Primary Training my instructor climbed out on the wing with the reassuring message: "I got . . . two kids. I want to stay alive. . . . I'm gettin' off. I'll watch them down here."

I wasn't that good, but I wasn't that bad, and I got mad. I certainly wasn't thinking of the top-hatted skull when I shoved the throttle all the way to the fire wall and was in the air before I knew it. In fact, while it flew with me on every flight for over three years, I never even thought about it until the day I lost it.

The war was over and we were all counting points to see if we could go home. I was still two points short, stuck in Japan and with too little to do because there were few planes in shape to fly. Most of the experienced crew chiefs had already gone Stateside. And there was a rumor that our new mechanics were refugees from Cook's and Baker's School. While pondering that information, I lost my little black-hatted skull.

Now, with no one shooting at me, my biggest danger seemed to be from poor maintenance or mechanical failure. To buy the farm after living through a whole war seemed ludicrous, and suddenly I decided that I needed all the luck I could get. Because I knew that I'd be flying the next day, I went to Tokyo to find a substitute for my little skull. There were no black-hatted skulls, so I had to settle for a small, carved ivory Japanese "god of death." At the time, I considered this a very appropriate substitute for my missing talisman.

The next day I took off from Tachikawa in a brand new C-46 with a full load of passengers and headed for Manila. About 200 miles south of Japan, at 9,000 feet, my right engine went out. The C-46 had power and could manage on one engine, and after a futile attempt to restart, I did a 180, headed back to the mainland of Japan. At about 7,000 feet, the left engine went out. This was an event to water my eyes, since the "big ass" bird, as the -46 was affectionately named, wasn't worth a damn as a boat.

I started searching for some land, anything solid to swim to, when the plane gave up trying to be a boat. A small volcanic protuberance stuck out of the water about a mile ahead. There was nothing else in sight. I lined up on this dot of dirt and planned to ditch right beside it. At 3,000 feet everything was ready for ditching, and as I started to glide toward the selected spot, I just happened to look down at the ivory god on my zipper. I ripped it loose, and threw it out the window with the comment, "You little bastard, you're not doing me any good."

As I opened my hand, both engines started again; the crew chief had decided to give it one more try. I kept those throttles open and headed back to Tachikawa as fast as she would go.

Once unloaded, I enlisted the help of the line chief, and with my own crew chief we took those engines apart. Because it was a relatively new plane, both engines were as clean and bright as a new watch. At that point I made a decision. Having flown all that time over the North American continent and the Pacific from Australia to Japan, I must have used up the luck that had resided in my black-hatted skull. With that lost, it was time to quit. So I did. The next day I received orders to go home with the option of piloting a C-46. Instead, I chose to spend 14 days on a Liberty ship to get to Seattle, plus three more on a troop train to get to Fort Dix, New Jersey, and out. I never really considered myself superstitious, but neither would I tempt fate! Years later I heard the rest of the story.

Sitting on a beach in Connecticut 25 years hence, I was telling of my lost talisman to an old college chum, who was by then a pilot but who had been a B-17 gunner in World War II. A gentleman who was sitting nearby apparently overheard the conversation, and he asked that I repeat the story, assuring me that he had a very good reason for the request. After I had gone over it again, he identified himself as having been at that time the Pratt & Whitney representative on the R 2800 engine in the Pacific. He said that if he had met me at that time, it might have saved him some work, for he had spent months looking for C-46 pilots who were having the same type of unexplained engine failure. Eventually, the trouble was traced to moisture forming on the ignition ring under changing humidity conditions over water, which shorted the plugs.

Nothing was said of talismans or luck, and from that point on I could truly claim that I was not superstitious. After our talk on the beach, I've flown many times since, usually with my CFII (certified flight instructor — instrument) son and without misgivings. Still, I wonder, what did happen to my little black-hatted skull?

Unwinding

As the end of my odyssey approached, things happened in the clouds of anticipation and wonder. What would come next? And what would be expected back in the world of civilian life? Excerpts of the last days may illustrate the nature of the transition.

18 October 1945
Tachikawa, Japan

Dear Mom,

. . . I've been busy seeing Japan and not flying, but still it took a lot of my time which I should have used for writing letters.

I've been in all the little towns and all over Tokyo and Yokohama. I've visited with the rich, poor and all classes for that matter. I've got a pretty good picture of Japan and now like everyone else, "I wanna go home." The prospects don't look so hot though.

Our ships have been flying food to Okinawa and we've had no mail in almost a month. Finally did get two letters today from you that were mailed just a month ago. The article mentioning the destruction of planes at Kanoya was interesting because 4 of those 13 C-46s were in our squadron and all were in our group.

I expect 3 months pay at the end of this month. They pay us in Jap money and since the standards are so different a couple of hundred bucks amounts to 10 lbs. of paper.

Nevertheless I intend to keep it for there are rumors which frankly I don't put much stock in to the effect that the group will fly the ships back next month. It's too good to be true, so I'm almost sure it will never be anything more than a rumor.

. . . I really don't know anything about how or when I'm getting home.

10 December 1945
Tachikawa, Japan

. . . We are getting in officers every day from other deactivated outfits — all with about the same service and time as I. The group needs about 200 officers to operate at full strength and it has close to 800. However, if they institute any service system everyone will be able to go home. I think they are stalling — just trying to figure a way to send some without sending all. It's a most sad setup no matter how you look at it.

I'm hoping we'll hear something favorable on Jan. 2. This inactivity is the most demoralizing thing you can imagine. I can manage OK but I'm certainly not enjoying it.

Your mail isn't coming very fast. It's being held up between the groups. I think the trouble is that they can't keep an EM [*enlisted man*] working on it long enough to locate us.

EMs are going home fast but not officers. We are practically as many as the day the war ended. Officers are beginning to out number EM when the ratio should be 20-1.

Goodbye for now. Hope I can see you soon.

13 March 1946
Tachikawa, Japan

. . . I'm still working in the dispensary (just finished sewing up a Jap's fingers). My flying is limited to 4 hours a mont' to get flight pay.

There is still no news as to when and how I can get home. The Okinawa battle star hasn't come through yet. They may drop service soon, perhaps the 15th to 40 months. That would catch me if it happens.

. . . I'm right on the borderline in points and service. Most of the older fellows have left and the newer ones coming to replace all seem like a bunch of kids. I suppose I acted that way a year or so ago myself, but honestly I have no patience with them anymore. I've yet to reach 22, but I feel ten years older. So much of everything seems just like "kid stuff" to me now.

. . . Yesterday they checked through our forms and added additional M.O.S.s [*Military Occupational Specialty*]. A good percentage have .0001, which means unassigned — in other words surplus but that means nothing regardless of orders from HQ to send all surplus men home. Still there is nothing to do but wait and hope.

Our mail is stopped both ways for a month because of lack of personnel to keep the planes flying. Now it's suppose to be cleared up. . . .

27 March 1946
Tachikawa, Japan

Just a short note to keep you abreast of things that aren't happening. As far as going home I don't know any more about it than when I last wrote. There is a story making the rounds saying that a surplus deal is going into effect which will make me eligible to leave as soon as all the 42 months men ship out. The catch seems to be shipping for these men have been processed for a month now and an article in *Stars & Stripes* said that all these men would not be cleared out before late May.

. . . Maybe with the coming of April something will be announced — a service or point drop.

. . . There are just no planes in flying condition. We now have a group of EM replacements, but they are all infantry, which doesn't help the flying end of it out at all.

Write all you can for letters mean a lot now and keep your fingers crossed for something may break soon — I hope.

28 March

P.S. I am clearing the field again today — processing tomorrow. Surplus 34 months and 50 points. Now it looks like a question of just waiting for a boat — That could be a month more easily. DO NOT STOP WRITING UNTIL I TELL YOU I'M GETTING ON THE BOAT. Something else may come up to keep me longer, though for the life of me I can't imagine what else they can dream up.

27 April 1946
Tachikawa, Japan

Well the Navigators and Bombardiers left yesterday but still no news of when the pilots are leaving. No one can understand why the navigators have been sent first since their requirements were lowest of all — only 24 months and 27 points. The rumors have put our leaving date as Monday, but there are no boats in as yet so I can't possibly see how that can be true. Everyone's afraid that this Russian scare is what is making them delay so long for once they do let us go, they will have lost all their old pilots. [*On 5 March 1946, Winston Churchill delivered his Iron Curtain speech as the first official warning of Soviet duplicity.*] However, I don't see how they can keep us since they have gone this far already. I really do expect to leave before the end of next week but you can never predict what the Army will do. You can only be sure that it's never logical.

No mail from either of you for so long that I've lost count. I guess you must have both decided that I was on my way home even though I cautioned you that processed didn't always mean a lot. I'll let you know as soon as something definite happens. Till then don't get all excited.

Take care of yourself and I'll see if I can't make it soon — as if I had any thing to say about it.

4 May 1946 41st T.C.Sq. 317th Grp.
Tachikawa, Japan

Got a letter from you the other day in which you were so sure that I was on my way home that you hardly thought that I could possibly be here to get it. Well that was four days ago and as you see I'm still here. We are still getting rumors that we will leave by the 14th. The strongest one is that there will be a Victory ship loading us on the 10th and [*the*] *General* . . . loading the balance on the 12th. It sounds pretty good and may be true for a change. The funny thing is that a Victory ship leaving two days earlier will get there after the *General* . . . since a Victory takes 14 to 18 days while [*the*] *General* . . . does it in 9 or 10. However, I'll get on the first one as I'd rather feel sure that I'm on the way than sit around wondering.

I hope you used your cleverness on Easter and on Bert's birthday [*30 April*] by getting her flowers from me. I didn't forget her birthday but I didn't tell you for at the time I felt sure I'd be home. Now I'm not sure of anything so don't count on my getting home by June 1 — just hope for and it may happen.

Keep your fingers crossed and we will see.

The *General* . . . did sail on 14 May into the strongest, four-day storm the ship's captain had seen in his 30 years at sea. Everyone, including the crew, was seasick except the flying personnel, who maliciously ate ham sandwiches in front of the sailors, just to be mean.

It arrived in Seattle on 26 May.

Almost 50 years later, a paper I prepared on group therapy still contains residuals from that time:

> Since the topic of men in groups has been considered, I feel constrained to add some data from my own personal life, where requisite time was spent in the tree house, the locker room, and the military barracks. I can never remember being puzzled for long as to what men around me were feeling. The idea that they don't express themselves is a myth. What they don't do is behave with peers as though they were in a polite, mixed society. Anger comes out as "son of a bitch" and sometimes a right cross. Romance, or more typically lust, is discussed openly in anatomical terms. Friendships are cemented in mutual intellectual and manual endeavors, recognized by others for the efficiency of the final product. And they cry, express fear, tenderness, and devotion, but usually only to those who earn their complete trust. In many ways men's feelings are deeper because they husband them. The idea that limited emotional expression occurs because men are conditioned to hide their feelings is simplistic in the extreme. For men the context in which the expression occurs is crucial and typically determines how feeling is displayed.

I recall being in a movie theater in Seattle, Washington, after debarking from the ship, as I together with most of the audience were in the process of getting reaccustomed to life Stateside. On the beaches and in the jungles of the Pacific, movies had been projected on screens usually set up in the open, and sometimes in the rain. First-run classics were not common, and what was available was often a rerun, so often in fact that the GIs memorized the scripts. To enhance the experience, new lines were introduced by shouting over the actors' lines. Whole new plots were group concocted to be lost on the winds of time. But, back in the civilian world, viewing Rita Hayworth in *Gilda* opened a floodgate of creative fantasies in this sex-starved audience. The air was blue with colorful sexual references, all designed to bypass the preliminaries and get Rita bedded. As it is with any group, the crudest and most candid members set the tone, but there was certainly no lack of expressed feelings.

And so it was, getting back to the real world — there were movies, cold milk, fresh meat, and the freedom to do pretty much what we liked, while awaiting transport to the East Coast.

Once again, there was the troop train and the prospect of three-plus days in transit. All passengers had been overseas for two to three years and all had but one goal — get home!

There were rumors that a railroader's strike was in the offing and that the train crews might just refuse to work. We veterans were in no way sympathetic with the rail workers' concerns, which threatened to interfere with our return home. Paratroopers, who still kept jump knives in their boots, talked of cutting a few throats, if necessary, to reach the East Coast. A more benign approach was proposed when three combat types, who were former railroad engineers, offered to "drive the damn train."

How was I aware of all the intrigue? I got stuck with the job of train commander. Thinking back to my first train trip under military orders, I had to ponder the irony, for as my military experience had begun on a troop train, so was it to end on one.

Obviously, all the rules of deportment initially enforced on naive enlistees would have been considered ridiculous by combat-tested veterans. I proposed but one rule: "Don't fall off the train, because we won't stop to pick you up."

Fortunately, before more drastic measures were needed to get us on our way, President Truman ordered that the trains keep running, strike or no strike.

I recall very little of the details of the trip, but I do remember Chicago. After two days on the train, we pulled into the rail yards. There I was told that future connections to the East were uncertain, but that we could count on at least an eight-hour delay. To keep men confined in the coaches for that long a period would have led to a riot. Thus, I issued six-hour passes with the warning that if anyone hadn't returned in time, he would be left in Chicago and charged with being AWOL. Within the six hours, they began returning, some with a little too much to drink, supported (carried) by their buddies; some with girlfriends that they had acquired (who were allowed to stay until we departed). But we were still short 250 men. Since I had expected that, I had requisitioned the services of an entire MP platoon, which was dispatched to round up our lost sheep. By the time that we actually pulled out, ten hours later, all but 50 had been located and returned, which represented less than ten percent of the entire bunch — not a bad record, and an index of how anxious they were to get home.

At Fort Dix we faced out-processing. We could wait for a complete physical or just sign a waiver and leave.

I accepted my "Ruptured Duck" discharge pin and left, catching the first train to New York and stepping back into the civilian world where my wife was waiting.

We had a second honeymoon in the same hotel where the first had occurred, this time without the specter of imminent overseas deployment.

My first two weeks at home were financed by the "Fifty-two, twenty club," which was a government stipend of $20 a week for 52 weeks, if you didn't find work. Supposedly, this gave veterans time to decompress. I put up with no work for a week and a half and then found a job — but that's the beginning of another story and another time.

Epilogue

Now, 50 years later, some things have remained the same, but much seems different.

As a psychologist I have treated veterans from World War II, Korea, Vietnam, and Iraq. The sameness was in their reports of the experiences of sheer terror, feeling helpless in the face of overwhelming odds imposed by the enemy and/or the laws of physics. From every war, I heard about the anger and confusion generated by poor leadership and the incompetence of superiors. Too often, the anguish resulted from the decisions of those in high places, who had no understanding of the actual combat situation. Tampering from the top was minimal in World War II, increased in Korea, and produced disaster in Vietnam. Iraq was the exception, perhaps reflecting the lesson learned in Nam, but now, with the precipitous decline of congressional members with military experience, the best prediction is that in a future conflict, politicians will be ignorant once again and try micromanagement.

As has always been the case, courage is an individual matter that takes many forms, as a situation demands. The men that I have treated from all wars expressed guilt because they had survived, while so many comrades perished — from the 2nd lieutenant who bailed out of a B-25, still wondering if everyone was really dead before he left the plane, to the Marine who won the Navy Cross, cursing because he had fired too many bursts from his machine-gun, such that there wasn't enough ammunition to save a friend who was being overrun by three Viet Cong. He had to use his .45 to dispatch the last one — too late. Each was the same in that he was committed to doing the job and to courageously protecting his buddies. So it is.

Combat can bring out the best in men, but it also often kills the best.

During World War II, the public seemed to understand and to care about husbands, sons, brothers, neighbors, and even strangers; but as the action escalated in Vietnam, too many civilians who opposed our involvement turned on the servicemen rather than the politicians. In that period, wives of some of my military patients received threatening phone calls, and men whose histories indexed sacrificial exploits beyond the call of duty would not wear the uniform in public to avoid vilification by individuals without the capacity to survive an overnight hike with a Boy Scout patrol. Post Traumatic Stress Disorder became the current euphemism, not only for being unable to recover from terrorizing experiences, but also for being unable to ignore the malicious behavior of one's fellow citizens.

In every case, my veteran patients believed that they fought to protect the rights of free speech, and they did not object to protests against the Vietnam involvement. Yet they could not fathom why *they* became the targets of venom, while it was acceptable for Jane Fonda to be pictured perched on a North Vietnamese anti-aircraft gun.

Somehow, in the time between World War II and the Vietnam war, an idea developed that those in the services welcome combat. Nothing could be further from the truth, for even in training, accidents occur and friends die.

Those who have been in battle learn to avoid it, while civilians don't have that opportunity. As observed by Medal of Honor recipient General James H. Howard in his *Roar of the Tiger*:

> There is nothing so transient in the minds of the public as military heros or the wars they fought. After the ticker tape parades and the dinner cliches, they become mere statistics. . . . Memories fade away and the world resumes its course as if nothing happened. . . .

For me, memories have faded somewhat, hence the foregone is full of gaps. And as we all must do, I've repressed the fear and pain of those years. I've recalled how we held it all together. What remained may seem too lighthearted, at times even frivolous, but laughter and tears are often interchangeable in the face of adversity.

Take Off

We lie in dreams of peace and home;
The waning moon sinks low,
And stars above wink sleepy eyes
On the quiet world below.

Nights like this were made for man
To dream of cool arms, warm lips.
Not protesting, screeching, diving planes
And burning, blasted ships.

But relentlessly, the moon moves on,
A glow in eastern sky
The mists like curling phantoms rise.
Our dreams are but a sigh.

A throaty, roaring blasting sound
Breaks upon God's cool dawn:
The battle planes are waiting.
The time for dreams is gone.

We fumble into flying clothes,
Strap guns around our waists.
Cool arms, warm lips forgotten,
This is the time for haste.

Hot coffee, searing black
Goes burning down our throats.
Do dreams really die
Or can they live in hopes?

The planes are waiting ready,
Eagles, eager for the fray.
As the last fading star
Foretells the coming day.

The runway lights flash on now,
A bright arrow pointing straight,
Toward assassins of peace and dreams,
Who have soiled the world with hate.

A blast of power, a whine of props,
And we are soaring high.
Once again we see that fading star,
Dropping from the sky.

White and clear, pure and bright,
It guides us on our way.
Our hope and dreams, there still;
Fast being hidden in the day.

How many dawns are there to be
Before this nightmare ends
And we come back to cooling arms,
Warm lips and loving friends?

JRL, *ca.* SWPA

Appendix A

Assignments

The problem here is one of memory. In that war no time was spent on paperwork. For some months I never knew from day to day where the Group or Squadron HQs were located, while I changed islands almost daily. Officially, for a time, Squadron HQ was at Nadzab, New Guinea; Tanuan, Leyte; Clark Field and Lingayen, Luzon; Ie Shima, Okinawa; Iwo Jima. I have no idea when the transfers occurred, but we always moved closer to Japan.

Atlantic City, New Jersey	Basic Training, 74th Training Wing, 710th Training Group, Army Air Forces Training Command (AAFTC)
Gettysburg, Pennsylvania	55th College Training Detachment, AAFTC
Nashville, Tennessee	Squadron F-3, Nashville Army Air Classification Center, AAFTC

Montgomery, Alabama	Squadron 3, Field IX, Army Air Forces Preflight Center, Maxwell Field, AAFTC
Union City, Tennessee	Primary Flight Training, Squadron D, Embry Riddle Field, AAFTC
Newport, Arkansas	Basic Flight Training, Cadet Detachment (Class 44-E), Newport Army Air Field, AAFTC
Blytheville, Arkansas	Advance Flight Training, Squadron C, Class 44-E, Blytheville Army Air Field, AAFTC
Alliance, Nebraska	1st Troop Carrier Command
Lawrenceville, Illinois	George Field; 1st Troop Carrier Command
Fayetteville, North Carolina	Pope Field; Pathfinder Training
Fort Wayne, Indiana	Baer Field; port embarkation
Fairfield, California	Travis Field; overseas shipping
Pearl Harbor, Hawaii	Hickham Field
Biak, New Guinea	Replacement Depot
Nadzab, Papua New Guinea	433rd Troop Carrier Group, 5th AF
Morotai, Celebes Sea	" " " " " "
Peleliu, Philippine Sea	" " " " " "
Tanuan, Leyte, PI.	" " " " " "
Clark Field, Luzon, PI.	" " " " " "

Lingayen, Luzon, PI.	433rd Troop Carrier Group, 5th AF
Ie Shima, Okinawa	" " " " " "
Iwo Jima	" " " " " "
Atsugi, Japan	" " " " " "
Tachikawa, Japan	375th Troop Carrier Group & 317th Troop Carrier Group, 5th AF
Seattle, Washington	Port debarkation
Fort Dix, New Jersey	139th Battalion 11th Replacement Depot, Discharge

Appendix B

Military Record and Report of Separation Certificate of Service

1. Last Name — First — M.I.			2. Army Serial #	3. Grade	4. Arm	5. Comp.
LESTER	JOHN	R	0 831 964	lst LT	AC	AUS

6. Organization	7. Date Relief	8. Place of Separation
70TH SQUADRON 433RD TCG 5th AIR FORCE	Active Duty 23 July 46	Fort Dix, N.J.

9. Permanent Address	10. Date of Birth	11. Place of Birth
95 STEARNS ST. BRISTOL, CONNECTICUT	11 APR 24	INDIANAPOLIS, IND.

12. Address from which employment will be sought	13. color eyes	14. color hair	15. ht.	16. wt.	17. #Dep
SEE 9	HAZEL	BROWN	5'10"	157	2

18. Race	19. Marital Status	20. US Citizen	21. Civ.Occp.#
W N O	S M O (specify)	Y N	
X	X	X	STUDENT X-02

MILITARY HISTORY

Selective Service Data	22. Registered	23. local ss Board #	24. County & State	25. Home at time entry
	Y N			
	X			SEE 9

26. Dates Entry Active Duty
28 Oct.'42 (enlisted)
23 May '44 (commission)

27. Military Occupational Spec.No.
PILOT TWO ENGINE 1051

28. Battles and campaigns
AIR OFFENSIVE JAPAN NEW GUINEA WESTERN PACIFIC SOUTHERN PHILIPPINES LUZON RYUKYUS

29. Decorations and Citations
AIR MEDAL AMERICAN CAMPAIGN MEDAL ASIATIC PACIFIC CAMPAIGN MEDAL ARMY OF OCCUPATION MEDAL WORLD WAR II VICTORY MEDAL
DISTINGUISHED UNIT BADGE (oak leaf) PHILIPPINE LIBERATION (star)

30. Wounds received in action
NONE

31. Service Schools attended	32. Service outside CONUS & return		
	Depart	Destination	Arrival
CLASS #44E ADVANCE FLYING	9 MAR 45	A P TH	26 MAR 45
GETTYSBURG COLLEGE (C & D)			

33. Reason & Auth.for Separation			
RELIEF FROM ACTIVE DUTY RR			
1-1 DEMOB	14 MAY 46	USA	26 MAY 46

34. Current Tour of Active duty(com)						35. Education(years)		
Continental Service			Foreign					
Yrs.	Mon.	Days	Yrs.	Mon.	Days	Gram.	Hs.	College
0	11	13	1	2	17	8	4	1\2

INSURANCE NOTICE

36. Kind ofIs. Nat Ser	37. How pd? Allot	38. Effective disc.	39. next Pre.	40. due	41. Int Cont.
X	X	31 JUL 46	31 AUG 46	$6.50	X

42. Right Thumb Print

43. Remarks
ASR SCORE (2 SEP 45) 62
PILOT
ON TERMINAL LEAVE FROM 5 JUN 46 TO 23 JUL 46 INCLUSIVE
LAPEL BUTTON ISSUED

44. Sign.of Off.Being Separated

45. Personnel Officer

MELVIN O MILLER
1st LT QMC

[*Document Presented to State of Connecticut. World War II Bonus*]

Index

By Lori L. Daniel